THE LIFE AND TEACHING OF JESUS

Books by
EDWARD W. BAUMAN
Published by The Westminster Press

Intercessory Prayer
The Life and Teaching of Jesus

THE LIFE
AND TEACHING
OF
JESUS

BY

Edward W. Bauman

Philadelphia
THE WESTMINSTER PRESS

LIBRARY OF CONGRESS CATALOG CARD No. 60–7038

PRINTED IN THE UNITED STATES OF AMERICA

For Audree

Contents

Preface

JESUS is a stranger in the midst of his own people. This is at once the tragedy of the modern church and the explanation for much of its lamented weakness. Christians talk about Jesus, sing about him, and offer prayer in his name, but do not know him. This fact can be verified by asking almost any group of church members a few basic questions about his life, teaching, death, and resurrection. I have done this many times under a variety of circumstances, and the results have been appalling without exception. We proudly bear the name of Christ, but we do not really know who he was or what he said and did.

There is no substitute for reading the Gospels as a way of learning these basic facts about Jesus, but unfortunately the Gospels are not always easy to read or understand. Their vocabulary is strange to our ears, their world strange to our eyes, and their religious ideas alien to our own experience. Hence the continuing need for orderly interpretive studies of the ministry of Jesus as a supplement to the Gospels. Hence also the reason for the utterly incredible success of a thirty weeks' television series on the life and teaching of Jesus, presented in the nation's capital.

This was the subject chosen for the first college-credit course to be offered over commercial television in the Washington area. In the late autumn of 1958, amid the flood of releases that pour out of this " news capital of the world," there appeared a notice of a college course in religion to be offered over television. The news was greeted with some enthusiasm, but loud voices of protest were also heard. In view of Washington's strategic position in world affairs, many persons insisted that college-credit television here should begin with courses on world politics, international affairs, or political philosophy. There was genuine fear that a course in religion would fail, thus jeopardizing the future of educational television in Washington. " Who," they wanted to know, " would take a full hour out of thirty Saturdays to watch a religious program? "

Then an amazing thing happened! After the first two or three programs, hundreds of people sent in registration fees and signed up for the course. Thousands more called or wrote enthusiastic letters. Bookstores sold out of the textbooks. An announced field trip was so heavily attended that special police were called out to handle the traffic. The ratings continued to climb, finally indicating that forty to eighty thousand people were watching each week, all of this during the noon hour on Saturday when a multitude of other interests bid for the time of busy Washingtonians.

Equally surprising were the increasingly favorable press notices that the course received. The television critics in *The Washington Post* and *The Washington Star* enthusiastically supported the series from the beginning. The United Press sent the story out on its wire service, and then letters came in from all parts of the world from those who wanted to know more about what was happening. Even *Variety,* the " Bible " of show business, published a lengthy article trying to account for the unexpected popularity of the program.

The most enthusiastic supporters of the project were unprepared for the growing interest that continued through the full thirty weeks. Beneath their very busy and sophisticated exterior, Washingtonians revealed an interior hunger to learn more about the Bible and especially about Jesus. Viewers came from every walk of life — young people and old, active businessmen and shut-ins, a mother with five small children and a grandfather with nineteen grandchildren, military generals and enlisted men, college professors and medical doctors, policemen and firemen, day laborers and United States Congressmen — these and countless others assured us of their continuing interest in the program. Comments gleaned from their letters and conversations would make a fascinating volume on the religious mind of modern America.

How can we account for the phenomenal success? Obviously the subject chosen is the principal explanation, for there is a contagious and self-authenticating quality about the life and teaching of Jesus that arouses a desire to know more. Persons caught up in the breathless rush and futility of modern living want to learn more about the eternal " good news " of the Gospels. This hunger is so deep that when the knowledge was made available on television many missed lunch, postponed trips to the shore, and even purchased television sets for the first time in order to gain new understanding.

In view of this longing to know more about Jesus, it is tragic that his life has often been hidden behind a cloud of dogmatic exclusiveness and theological obscurantism. Knowing that such an approach would be suicidal on television, we tried to develop a simple, direct, nonsectarian method of presentation. This method was clearly stated in the course outline: " Our purpose is to discover what can be known of the life of Jesus of Nazareth and his message. The approach will make use of scholarly material now available in many fields, including the new light shed on Biblical studies by the Dead Sea scrolls. It will be nonsectarian, and alternative views will be presented on important points where there are serious differences of opinion."

This book has been written in response to thousands of requests from those who were swept up in the excitement of this direct and orderly study of the message and mission of Jesus. In the following pages I have attempted to record the essence of the

life and teaching of Jesus as presented over TV in this incredibly
successful series. The atmosphere of the original presentation may
be missing to some extent, since certain vital features must be
omitted. The National Gallery of Art, for example, the Smith-
sonian Institution, and other resources made rich visual contributions to our programs. The heated debates among the college students present in the studio each week also aroused a great deal of
interest among the viewers. But even with such " live " features
missing, it is still possible to present the heart of the matter in
direct, simple, systematic form.

The book is intended for the general reader as well as the
careful student. The suggested reading list makes it possible to
use this material on many different levels as a guide to understanding Jesus. The casual reader will find here the simple basic
facts out of which the Christian religion grew, while the more
careful student will be able to use Biblical and additional reading
references to ferret out of these simple facts their deeper impli-
cations.

Never before in the history of mankind has the study of the
life of Jesus been more vital and rewarding. In an age of anxiety
and despair when man's very existence is threatened, the ministry
and message of Jesus speak more clearly than ever of God's purpose for man and the world. Amid the chaos and confusion of
our time there is new evidence of man's hidden hunger for this
good news of God in Jesus.

EDWARD W. BAUMAN

Washington, D.C.

"But who do you say that I am?"

INTRODUCTION

1

The World of Jesus

EVERYONE knows that Jesus influenced the world. Few people stop to consider how the world influenced Jesus. We are often told how he made a greater impact on history than " all the armies that ever marched and all the parliaments that ever sat." But we seldom hear how his ministry was shaped and influenced by marching armies and political turmoil in his own time. He did not live in a cultural vacuum, but in the midst of a teeming civilization with a long and honored tradition. We cannot understand his life and teaching without knowing something of this civilization and this tradition.

One of the unique facts about Christianity is that the revelation of God in Jesus was this kind of historical revelation, occurring at a particular time and place in the life of a particular people. Philosophers and theologians have often wondered why God chose to reveal himself most fully in this way. But the fact is that he did, and, therefore, any mature appreciation of the person in whom he revealed himself must include some knowledge of the world in which he lived. Fortunately, this study has been receiving increasing attention, stimulated by the discovery of the Dead Sea scrolls. It is becoming increasingly evident that the more we know of the world of Jesus, the more we can know of Jesus himself.

There is always a temptation, however, to plunge into the study of Jesus at some advanced point in his life. It should be emphasized, therefore, that those who patiently master the background material will make the greater progress. As Aristotle once said, "Those who wish to succeed must ask the right preliminary questions." The right preliminary question for those who wish to know Jesus is the question of what the world was like in which Jesus lived.

A. The Country

Palestine is a country about the size of the state of New Hampshire located on the eastern shore of the Mediterranean Sea. Though small in size, it is a land of great natural beauty and of wide contrast and variety. Jesus would have known both the mountain country of upper Galilee, including snow-clad Mt. Hermon, and the subtropical Jordan Valley. He was also very much at home on the little Sea of Galilee as well as in the villages along the shore. He spoke often of the trees, flowers, animals, wind, and weather of the little country he knew so well. The natural beauty of Palestine made it an ideal location for a religious ministry whose emphasis was on the goodness of God.

Topographically, Palestine consists of four parallel bands running north and south: (1) A narrow coastal plain runs along the shore of the Mediterranean, fertile enough for agricultural development and level enough to serve as a highway for the armies of great empires. (2) The central hill country constitutes the bulk of the inhabited area. Orchards, vineyards, and grazing sheep abound in the open spaces between the many villages that dot the countryside. (3) The Jordan Valley, created by the famous river of song and legend, is filled with thick tropical vegetation. The muddy river empties into the salty Dead Sea. (4) The wilderness of Transjordan ("across the Jordan"), a desolate plateau, figures in the Gospel story only as a place of retreat.

Palestine in the first century was divided into three distinct political regions: (1) Galilee in the north was the homeland of

Jesus. The name means " circle of the Gentiles," a constant reminder of the fact that it was not populated with Jews until about
one hundred years before the birth of Jesus. The inhabitants were
noted for their " Galilean accent," and for their sturdy independence of spirit. Most of the Zealots, those interested in insti-
gating a political revolution, came from Galilee. The countryside
was fertile and heavily cultivated, Josephus calling it " the garden
of Palestine." Important landmarks in Galilee are Nazareth,
Capernaum, and the Sea of Galilee. (2) Samaria, in the central
part of the country, is an area of many vineyards and orchards.
The Samaritans were the descendants of the Jews and Assyrians
who had intermarried following the fall of Samaria in 721 B.C.
The Bible emphasizes that " the Jews had no dealings with
the Samaritans," largely because the Samaritans claimed to be the
true representatives of Israel. (3) Judea, in the south, was the
center of Judaism. At the center of Judea was the great city of
Jerusalem and at the center of Jerusalem stood the magnificent
Temple. The inhabitants of Judea were proud of their pure Jewish descent and of the central place that Jerusalem occupied in
the life and thought of Judaism. Other Judean cities mentioned
in the Gospels are Bethlehem and Jericho.

The climate of Palestine is somewhat similar to southern Cali-
fornia. A great deal of discomfort could be caused by hot winds
off the desert and sudden storms on the Sea of Galilee, but for
the most part Palestine was ideally suited to a man who loved
nature and who had " nowhere to lay his head."

The strategic location of Palestine is a key factor in the history
of Judaism and Christianity. Sir George Adam Smith called the
little country " the bridge of Asia," thus emphasizing its place
at the center of the overland route between the two main centers
of civilization in this part of the ancient world. The Jewish homeland is located on the southwestern tip of the Fertile Crescent, a
crescent-shaped area of land with one tip in the Tigris-Euphrates
valley and the other in the Nile basin. The history of Israel in a

real sense is the history of marching armies and heavily laden caravans passing through this crossroads of the ancient world. It is a serious mistake to think of Jesus' homeland as an out-of-the-way country, cut off from the main currents of his time, for Palestine was in many ways one of the important centers of the ancient world.

B. ECONOMIC FACTORS

The economic situation in the world of Jesus is seldom emphasized enough in studies of his life. Certainly poverty and economic unrest were key factors in the historical drama that gave birth to Christianity. It is unusually difficult for most of us to feel our way into this situation of extreme poverty because our standard of living is so high, but in the Palestine that Jesus knew the majority of people were always on the verge of economic disaster. Many of them went to bed at night not knowing whether they would eat on the morrow. For them the prayer of Jesus would be very real, " Give us this day our daily bread."

Many occupations were represented in the economic life of Palestine. There were craftsmen, fishermen, merchants, government officials, and people of wealth. Basically, however, it was an agricultural nation with every available piece of land under cultivation. Most of the farmers were small landowners, working long hours to eke out a hand-to-mouth kind of existence. Under ideal conditions life would have been tolerable, but there were two factors that made life difficult. One was the marginal type of living which meant that poverty was never very far away. A severe illness or a season of drought could result in economic ruin. The other factor that made life difficult, if not intolerable, was the double system of taxation, Jewish and Roman.

The Jews were heavily taxed for support of their national religion, paying tithes of their crops and making countless offerings for such things as first-born children, animals, the poor, the Temple, synagogues, priests, and rabbis. An even greater burden of assessments was imposed by Rome. Rabbi Klausner has discovered evidence of the following: a poll tax, a salt tax, a crown tax (crowns of the bride and bridegroom), a land tax, a cattle tax, a tax on fruit trees, an annual tax, a sales tax, a water tax, a city tax, a road tax, a house tax, and a frontier tax (customs). The total may have been 40 per cent or more of a man's total income. The whole system was aggravated by graft and corruption, for the taxes were collected by political appointees who tried to get a share of the spoils.

The revolutionary tension caused by this economic unrest was without doubt one of the decisive factors in shaping the lives of the people in Jesus' world. Many angry and embittered persons, such as Judas of Galilee who led an unsuccessful revolt early in the century, plotted the overthrow of the government. "No tribute to Rome!" was his battle cry. Other persons, however, waited quietly for God to intervene, certain that when the situation became intolerable he would send his Messiah to inaugurate a kingdom in which there would be economic prosperity for all. It was not unusual for banquet scenes to be included in the descriptions of God's coming kingdom. As modern communists have demonstrated anew, poverty and economic unrest are breeding grounds for revolutionary change. This was certainly true of Palestine in the first century.

Those who feel the tension of this economic situation will come to a new appreciation of many factors in the life and teaching of Jesus. We can see the relevance of Peter's question to Jesus about the Temple tax, and the question of Jesus' enemies, "Is it lawful to pay taxes to Caesar?" Moreover, the temptation for a man of compassion to do something about this economic need must have been almost overwhelming at times. It is not surprising that the first temptation that came to Jesus in the wilderness was that of turning stones into bread — becoming an economic Messiah and satisfying the hunger that dominated the lives of so many people. Jesus rejected this temptation for something higher, but ever present economic factors must be included in any full appreciation of his developing ministry.

C. POLITICAL FACTORS

In the realm of politics also Palestine was tinder dry, waiting for the spark to set off a full-scale revolution. Jesus, caught up in this tense atmosphere, was killed as a revolutionary shortly after his ministry began. Many of his actions and many of the things he said, especially about his own Messianic ministry, become meaningful only when viewed in the framework of this political situation.

For many centuries the land of Israel had been a pawn in the power struggle between great empires. In Old Testament times the Hebrew people were caught between Assyria, Babylonia, and Persia (in succession) on one side and Egypt on the other. The armies of these mighty powers marched back and forth through the little land, often leaving a wake of pillage, death, and destruction. More than once the people had seen their farms destroyed, their families broken up, their leading citizens carried off into exile. " By the waters of Babylon, there we sat down and wept," lamented the psalmist. The people had long known such weeping.

Then came the Hellenistic era, beginning with Alexander the Great in the late fourth century. During this period, Greek culture spread rapidly across the ancient world. Every land knew the march of Alexander's armies and felt the impact of Hellenistic art and ideas. The New Testament itself is written in Greek and contains much evidence of Greek influence (cf. the Gospel of John). Under the successors of Alexander an attempt was made to stamp out the Jewish religion, replacing it entirely with Hellenism, but this was too much for the Jews. They rebelled in 167 B.C. and gained a century of precarious independence, until, in 63 B.C. Pompey marched into Jerusalem at the head of the conquering Roman legions.

During the lifetime of Jesus, Rome ruled the ancient world. The long and peaceful reign of Augustus Caesar (30 B.C. to A.D. 14) was the high-water mark of Roman prosperity. Readers of Luke's Gospel will recognize this ruler, for it was a decree from Caesar Augustus that caused Joseph to take the long journey from Nazareth to Bethlehem with the expectant Mary at his side.

Roman policy allowed a good deal of freedom for conquered people as long as they caused no trouble and paid their taxes. Herod the Great was thus appointed as a " puppet " king (40–4 B.C.) and was allowed to rule with an iron hand. The Jews hated him for his ruthlessness and treachery. He crushed his enemies, murdering friend and foe alike, including his own beloved wife and three of his sons because he suspected them of treason. The slaughter of the Bethlehem children is not at all out of character for such a man. The death of Herod, which finally came, was hailed by the Jews and celebrated as a festival of thanksgiving!

Palestine then was split into three sections and divided among Herod's surviving sons. The district to the north and east of Galilee was given to Philip. Galilee and Peraea were given to Herod Antipas, the Herod we encounter in the public ministry of Jesus. Judea was given to Archelaus, but revolution soon broke out and the region was taken over by Roman procurators who were more directly under the influence of Rome. Pontius Pilate was the most famous of the procurators, ruling from A.D. 26–36.

Down through the centuries the Jews had nourished their dream of independence. Under the heavy yoke of Rome, revolutionary tension increased from one end of the nation to the other. The country was filled with malcontents and Zealots whose slogan was, " The sword and not sparingly; no king but God! " Scarcely a year went by without wars and other disturbances. Spies were everywhere, so that it was dangerous to take sides in political matters. During the lifetime of Jesus, the people were becoming increasingly restless, so that talk of revolution and plans for revolution were a part of their daily conversation. The slightest spark might lead to an explosion.

Jesus had undoubtedly witnessed the execution of revolutionaries, for such scenes were common. He knew the danger of speaking about a kingdom other than Rome and he knew the danger of making Messianic claims. This is one reason why he chose his words so carefully and delayed so long in announcing his own Messianic calling. In the wilderness he had been tempted to become a military leader and crush the hated Romans, but he had rejected the temptation once and for all. His kingdom was not of this world. His friends misunderstood his intentions, however, and tried to force him to become a king, arguing over their own places in the future kingdom! Jesus lamented over Jerusalem and predicted the destruction of the Temple, for he knew that, when the revolution finally came, mighty Rome would crush it ruthlessly. As it turned out, Jesus was executed for treason, and the great rebellion broke out shortly thereafter. In A.D. 70, Jerusalem was laid to waste and the magnificent Temple destroyed, never to stand again. The ministry of Jesus becomes intelligible only when seen against this background of mounting revolutionary turmoil.

D. Religious Factors

Jesus was born into a pious Jewish home where he was nourished on the Jewish Scriptures. Later in his life he said that he had come to fulfill the law and the prophets of Judaism. The inscription placed on the cross on which he died identified him as "The King of the Jews." In view of these deep roots in the Jewish faith it is essential to understand the religious background out of which Jesus came.

Although the Old Testament emphasizes the importance of the patriarchs (Abraham, Isaac, Jacob), the history of Israel actually begins with the exodus from Egypt. The Hebrews in Egypt had been reduced to serfdom and sorely oppressed. Under the leadership of Moses, they were released by a reluctant Pharaoh who then changed his mind and decided to pursue them. At the Red Sea, as the armies of Egypt closed in on the helpless Hebrews, a wondrous thing happened. The Hebrews were saved and the Egyptians destroyed! From this moment the Hebrews looked upon themselves as a chosen people, chosen by God to enjoy special privileges and responsibilities and to assume a unique role in history. Under the leadership of Moses at Sinai, they entered into a solemn covenant (agreement) with God — he would be their God; they would be his people. The conditions of the covenant relationship were expressed in the law that described what God expected of his people. It would be difficult to over-emphasize the significance of this formative experience under the leadership of Moses. The whole of the later history of Israel, political as well as religious, is based on the exodus event and the fundamental covenant relationship that grew out of it.

After conquering the Promised Land, the Hebrews established a monarchy successively ruled by Saul, David, and Solomon. On the death of Solomon the little nation split into two smaller powers, the Northern Kingdom falling before Assyria in 721 B.C. and the Southern Kingdom before Babylonia in 586 B.C. Carried off into exile, the Jews finally returned to their homeland for a period of restoration under the benevolent Persians. Then, as we have already seen, the threat of assimilation during the next era led to a century of independence that was ended by the conquest of Rome.

During all these centuries of political confusion, the prophets tried to call the people back to an awareness of their covenant relationship to God. The chosen people were not supposed to be like the other nations, placing their faith in kings and in military power. But the people refused to listen, and their misery increased until there gradually emerged the firm conviction that God would intervene again as he had at the Red Sea. This time he would step in and send a Messiah, a great leader, who would re-establish the covenant relationship and initiate a glorious era of independence and economic plenty under the reign (king-dom) of God.

The religious beliefs that emerged out of these experiences were expressed in certain terms that play a prominent role in the re-ligion of the Old Testament and in the Gospels. Taken in order, they constitute a helpful summary of the Jewish faith.

Monotheism: The belief that there is only one God is the key-stone of the Jewish religion. This faith is summarized in the *Shema,* an affirmation recited daily by the pious Jew: " Hear, O Israel, the Lord our God is one Lord." This one God is creator of heaven and earth; he is righteous in his dealings with men; he is transcendent and holy. He reveals himself in many ways, but especially through history. This high and noble monotheism is one of the outstanding contributions of Judaism to the history of mankind.

Chosen People: The people of Israel believed that God had singled them out as divinely chosen objects of his favor. He had freely revealed himself to them in a unique way during the exo-dus experience. At first they emphasized their privileges as a chosen people and only later recognized their responsibility as a " light to the Gentiles."

Covenant: The covenant is the binding agreement between God and the chosen people. This agreement is binding on both parties: I will be their God, they will be my people. The exodus experience in which they felt God had chosen them and the covenant that followed together constitute the formative and definitive event in Israel's history.

The Law: Every covenant or agreement has certain stated con-ditions. The law states the conditions for the covenant between God and Israel. The Hebrew word " tōrāh " literally means " in-struction," instruction concerning God's will for man. In essence, the law describes the way of life for those who are in a covenant relationship with God. It includes everything a man does, both great and small. This law is found primarily in the first five books of the Old Testament, but came to include a large body of "tradition" concerning the details of daily living.

Sacrifice: Since men often broke the covenant relationship through disobedience to the law, some means of restoring this broken relationship was necessary. Sacrifice was the method whereby an individual or the nation healed the broken relationship with God. The animal was offered in place of the life of the one who offered it. The great prophets of Judaism believed that divine forgiveness was based on something deeper than the death of sacrificial victims, but the idea of sacrifice continued to play an important role in the Jewish faith, and later in the Christian interpretation of the death of Jesus.

The Temple: The building in which animal sacrifices were made was the Temple in Jerusalem. There was only one Temple, apparently a magnificent building devoted to sacrificial worship and prayer under the leadership of the priests and Levites, a lesser religious order. The Temple in Jerusalem was the national religious shrine of Judaism.

Synagogues: The word literally means "gathering of people" or "congregation." When the Jews were in exile, and thus separated from the Temple, they gathered in local groups to study and discuss the law and to pray. The synagogue, therefore, is not a place of sacrifice, but of worship, study, and prayer. Although many modern synagogues are called "temples," the New Testament student should carefully maintain the distinction between synagogues as places of study and worship and the one Temple in Jerusalem as the center of the sacrificial system.

Prophet: A prophet is "one who is inspired by God." His main function as a spokesman for God is in calling the people back to their covenant relationship, warning them against disobedience and unfaithfulness. The prophets were not primarily foretellers (predicting the future), but forthtellers (proclaiming God's will). Their task was to declare the will of God for a specific situation. Since the Jews believed that prophecy had ceased after the exile, there was great excitement among those who felt that Jesus might be one of the great prophets returned.

Kingdom of God: As we have seen, the Jews believed that God would intervene to end the intolerable misery of their earthly existence. First, there would come a period of woe and then the great judgment. This would be followed by the Kingdom of God. "Reign of God" and "age to come" were common terms referring to the same expectation. In the age to come, God's reign would be established with Israel as the world center and Jerusalem as the capital. The Kingdom of God became the central theme of Jesus' teaching.

Messiah: Some believed that God would soon intervene directly, but most persons expected him to send an agent, a messiah, who would inaugurate the reign of God. The Messiah ("the anointed one") was expected to be a descendant of the great King David. As a warrior-king he would destroy the enemies of Israel, judge the world, and establish God's rule. In view of this Messianic expectation it is not surprising that the ministry of Jesus caused so much excitement. Was he the expected One or must they wait for another?

Also important in the Judaism of the first century were the religious parties, or "ways of thinking." Josephus calls them "philosophies," but they are not philosophies in the usual sense. Their differences lay partly in social and economic status and partly in religious and political outlook.

Sadducees: These were the conservative, aristocratic, landowning priestly families whose life centered around the Temple in Jerusalem. Religiously, they were conservative, rejecting the traditions of the scribes and the doctrine of the resurrection, as we see in their conflict with Jesus. Hated by their fellow Jews because of their collaboration with Rome, they disappeared from history following the destruction of Jerusalem.

Pharisees: These were the middle-class substantial citizens, most of whom were devout and intelligent. The name means

" separated one." They separated themselves in order to observe the ritual purity of the law, believing that the law was perfect and permanent and that the purpose of life was absolute obedience. Among the Pharisees there were scribes who studied and interpreted the law and Zealots who were ready to lay down their lives in the struggle for freedom. Much maligned by many Christians, the Pharisees should be commended for their sincerity and zeal. Modern Judaism has descended in an unbroken line from the Pharisees of the first century. Unfortunately, however, many of their practices tended toward hypocrisy, formalism, and unimaginative legalism. The harshest recorded words of Jesus are directed against the hypocrisy of the Pharisees, his chief enemies.

People of the Land: The majority of the lower-class people did not belong to any formal party. Living quiet, often devout lives, they were looked upon with contempt by the Sadducees and Pharisees. Jesus ministered directly to this group (" the common people heard him gladly ") and apparently was counted one of them because of his failure to observe ritual purity.

Essenes: These were the farmer-monks who lived in isolated, communal, disciplined brotherhoods. They were noted for prayer, manual labor, strict discipline, continence, and white robes. Largely unknown before the discovery of the Dead Sea scrolls, there is now intense speculation about their relationship to John the Baptist and Jesus.

A survey of the economic, political, and religious aspects of the world of Jesus reveals one thing quite clearly. The time was ripe for the coming of a great leader. Economic need and political tension mingled with fervent religious hope for God's intervention. As the burden of Rome grew heavier, hopes for a Messiah grew stronger. All these factors were working together in creating a tense and expectant atmosphere.

Those who swim in the ocean know how the largest waves often hang suspended for a split second before crashing in a mighty roar of spray and foam. The wave of economic need, political unrest, and religious hope had been gathering strength for many generations. Just before the coming of Jesus it seemed to hang suspended, ready to crash in a thundering roar that broke the back of history and changed the course of man's future destiny. The fullness of time had come.

2

Available Sources

ONE of the surprising features of the life of Jesus is the scarcity of trustworthy primary sources. We might reasonably expect a multitude of reliable reports on the activities and words of one whose life did more to change the course of history than any other. Instead we find a most disconcerting lack of records. We know practically nothing at all about the first thirty years of his life, and the reports of his public ministry are so incomplete we do not know whether it lasted one year or three. Of the four primary sources, one is so at variance with the other three that we are at a loss to know which to accept. At times the student of the life of Jesus feels like Sherlock Holmes, basing vitally important conclusions on the merest shreds of firsthand evidence.

How can we account for this paucity of records? As far as non-Christians are concerned, Paul gives a clear explanation when he says that Jesus was foolishness to the Gentiles and a stumbling block to the Jews. The Gentiles would find it pure foolishness to believe that an unlettered teacher from an obscure little village would have any influence on history. Jewish thought, on the other hand, " stumbled " over the idea that the long-expected Messiah would die like a common criminal. Only the followers of Jesus would have any reason to write, but they wrote very little for several reasons: they believed the end of the world was coming; they were not literary-minded, coming generally from the uneducated classes; they had been reared in the Jewish tradition that placed the major emphasis on the spoken word; the immediate disciples were still living; writing materials were expensive. Those who wish to know more about Jesus are thus left with only four primary sources and a fervent wish that more had been written.

In view of this scarcity of trustworthy sources it is doubly important for the student to be able to handle the material at his disposal with intellectual facility and maturity. A great artist can fashion a masterpiece with little material if necessary, but he must know his material and his subject well. In order to make the record complete, we will look at the brief pagan and Jewish notices before turning to the chief primary sources, the Christian Gospels.

A. Pagan Sources

There are no pagan references to Jesus during the first century and only three brief notices shortly thereafter among the Roman writers whose works are known to us. These notices tell us little beyond the fact that a man named Christ had lived and that a movement had grown up among his followers.

Pliny, the Younger, was appointed governor of an outlying province and wrote to Emperor Trajan for advice on dealing with Christians (A.D. 111–115). He describes their simple habits of worship, their honest and pure ways of living, and their participation in a common meal. His account gives evidence of two kinds of Christians, the unfaithful who cursed Christ under pressure and the faithful who were martyred for their belief.

Tacitus, the aristocratic historian, described in his *Annals* (A.D. 116) the terrible fire in Rome in A.D. 64, and suggested that it had been set on orders from Nero who then blamed it on the Christians. He speaks of "Christus, the founder of the name," and has nothing good to say about Christianity, describing it as a loathsome disease.

Suetonius, the famous biographer, published his *Lives of the*

Caesars in A.D. 120. In his record of the reign of Claudius the following sentence occurs: " Since the Jews constantly made disturbances at the instigation of Chrestus, he [Claudius] expelled them from Rome." There is some debate about the spelling of Chrestus, but it is probably another form of Christus.

B. JEWISH SOURCES

The only reliable Jewish evidence about Jesus is found in Josephus and the Talmud. Discounting the slanderous comments and the later Christian interpolations, about all we learn from these sources is that Jesus was executed as a false teacher.

Josephus, the noted Jewish historian, moved to Rome after the fall of Jerusalem in A.D. 70 and wrote *The Antiquities of the Jews* for the benefit of Roman readers. He was wary of saying anything favorable about Jesus, so he confined himself to a few very general remarks that were later expanded by Christian editors. He concludes his notice by saying that when Jesus was crucified, " those who had loved him at first did not cease to do so. And the tribe of Christians so named from him are not extinct to this day."

The Talmud is an authoritative Jewish book containing a compilation of wisdom and tradition. Although the main body of this tradition comes from the first century, the few references to Jesus are slanderous, since he was the founder of a hated party. According to the Talmud, Jesus practiced sorcery, led Israel astray, mocked at the words of the wise, and was hanged as a false teacher on the eve of the Passover.

C. CHRISTIAN SOURCES

It should be obvious from the above summary of non-Christian sources that we are almost wholly dependent upon the Christian records for our knowledge of the life and teaching of Jesus.

There are certain noncanonical records, such as the Gospel of Thomas and the Gospel of Peter, that contain a good deal about

Jesus. Unfortunately, the bulk of this material is highly unreliable, consisting mostly of grotesque and fanciful stories and legends. Jesus, for example, as a little boy playing with clay sparrows suddenly turns them into lively chirping birds. Although these noncanonical sources had a wide influence in later Christian writing, they are of little value to those wishing to know about the Jesus who actually lived and taught in Palestine.

At first glance we might expect to learn a good deal about Jesus from the writings of Paul in the New Testament. As a contemporary of Jesus and one who knew the earliest disciples, Paul should be able to tell us a good deal. But Paul's interests were primarily doctrinal, not biographical. He was interested in the meaning of the life, death, and resurrection of Jesus, not in the facts themselves. For the most part he assumed that those to whom he was writing already knew the facts about Jesus from the oral tradition. He therefore concentrated in his writing on that which for him was the heart of the matter, the eternal meaning of the crucified and risen Christ.

Thus we find ourselves turning to the four canonical Gospels for almost all that can be known of the life and teaching of Jesus. Even here there are certain limitations, however, for it became obvious very early that the first three Gospels differed radically from John in form, content, and style. John often changes the order of events at crucial points as we see in the second chapter where the cleansing of the Temple comes at the beginning of the ministry. He omits certain vital events and sayings, such as the baptism, temptation, and transfiguration, and he adds others. The raising of Lazarus and the foot washing in the upper room appear only in John. For these and other reasons the Fourth Gospel is usually studied separately. We follow this practice here, reserving until Chapter 16 a detailed study of John.

The historical study of the life and teaching of Jesus is thus based primarily on Matthew, Mark, and Luke, three Gospels that have striking similarities of vocabulary, content, and order of events. Often they agree down to the punctuation, word order, and sentence structure. Because of this common point of view these Gospels are called the "Synoptic" Gospels, from a Greek word meaning "looked at together." The Synoptics, as they are often referred to, can be arranged in parallel columns and "looked at together," so that their amazing similarities become instantly apparent. An invaluable tool for the study of the life of Jesus is a copy of *The Gospel Parallels,* preferably in the Revised Standard Version.

The word "gospel," or "evangel," comes from a Greek word meaning "good news" or "good tidings." As used by Christians it means the good news of what God has done in Jesus Christ. God has taken the initiative in providing for the transformation of man's life through the act of reconciliation. The separation between God and man is overcome; man is reconciled to God when he turns in repentance to receive the forgiving love of God through Jesus Christ. The mighty act of God in Jesus Christ that makes this reconciliation possible is incredible good news to men wandering in the lonely winter of their estrangement from God. The Four Gospels are primarily the record of this gospel or good news as it was received and interpreted by the later followers of Jesus.

The earliest tradition or remembrance was in the form of oral accounts handed down by those who heard Jesus and knew him. Very early these oral accounts were written in fragmentary form and preserved, though without any attempt to keep them in order. Finally, around thirty years after the death of Jesus, the author of Mark's Gospel made the first attempt to gather the fragmentary remembrances about Jesus into a coherent narrative. Others wrote later, trying to improve or supplement Mark's work. The actual composition of the Gospels thus took many years, beginning as oral tradition, developing into written fragments, and ending with the work of editors or authors who collected and organized the material they received. The thirty-year period during which the gospel was handed down in the form of oral and written fragments may well account for many of the textual problems that arise in any serious reading of the Four Gospels.

Some of these problems, however, may also be caused by the relationship of the written Gospels to one another. Scholars have long been puzzled, for example, by the similarities and differences between the Synoptic Gospels. The attempt to account for these numerous similarities and differences is called " the Synoptic problem."

Evidence that gives rise to the problem may be summarized as follows: (1) Three sevenths of the material in these three Gospels is common to all three. This material, largely narrative, is called the " triple tradition " since it occurs in all three Gospels. The similarity includes content, word order, words used, and punctuation. (2) Two hundred verses are common to Matthew and Luke, but are not found in Mark. These verses, largely teaching material, are called the " double tradition." (3) The three Gospels are similar in their general outline, for the most part recording events in the same order. (4) Similar passages in the three Gospels often agree in their use of unusual words or harsh grammatical constructions. (5) In spite of these striking similarities, there are equally striking differences. Each Gospel contains material that the other two do not have, and there are some obvious discrepancies (cf. the genealogies of Jesus and the two versions of the Lord's Prayer). The problem that arises from such evidence may be stated as follows: " The Synoptic problem is to construct a theory that will account for the likenesses and differences of the first three Gospels by determining their relationship, sources, and chronological order."

Many possible solutions to the problem have been suggested. At first, scholars believed that all three Synoptics had copied from a common oral or written source. Various other documentary hypotheses were developed before B. H. Streeter in a famous book, *The Four Gospels,* proposed the four-document hypothesis. Although revision of Streeter's work has been necessary at many points, the four-document hypothesis is the best working basic theory for students of the life and teaching of Jesus. It may be diagramed as follows:

THE FOUR-DOCUMENT HYPOTHESIS

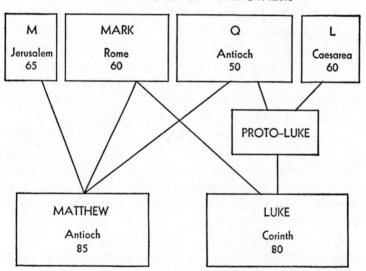

According to this hypothesis, Mark was the first Gospel written. Careful investigation shows that it is more primitive in language, literary form, and religious attitude. Streeter, moreover, gives five reasons to show why it is apparent that Matthew and Luke were dependent upon Mark. (1) They reproduce 90 per cent of Mark. (2) They follow Mark's outline. (3) Even when one strays from the common outline, Mark is the common denominator. (4) Mark's language is toned down or smoothed out at many points. (5) The form of Mark's writing is far more primitive than that of the other two.

The same tests that indicate that Matthew and Luke used Mark as a common source lead scholars to believe that the two hundred verses of double tradition come from another common source that emphasized the teaching of Jesus. The document itself has been lost to history, but attempts have been made to reconstruct it from Matthew and Luke. This document, called " Q " from the German word *Quelle* (" source "), accounts for the remarkable parallels of double tradition.

Matthew contains some material that is not found in any of the other Gospels, usually designated as the M source. Similarly, Luke had a special source, L, accounting for the material peculiar to his Gospel. From a study of the way in which Luke uses Mark it also seems probable that he had an early edition of his Gospel to which he later added the material from Mark. This early edition, made up of Q plus L, is called " proto-Luke."

In this way the four-document hypothesis accounts for the likenesses and differences of the first three Gospels. Mark was written first. Matthew is made up of Mark plus Q plus his own source, M. Luke first wrote a Gospel using Q plus L, then added Mark at a later date. This is called the four-document hypothesis because it is based on four primary documents, Mark, Q, M, and L.

Modern New Testament scholarship in dealing with the Synoptic problem has followed one of two possible routes. Some scholars have expanded Streeter's theory into a multiple-document hypothesis, insisting that there are many sources of written material used by the authors of the Synoptics. It is extremely difficult, however, to label these sources with any degree of accuracy.

Far more significant is the work of the form critics, those who try to discover the form of the tradition during the period of oral transmission. These scholars are certain that the sayings and actions of Jesus were remembered and transmitted from the beginning in certain fixed forms. These forms were treasured and polished, like pearls, until the editors of the Synoptics simply strung them into a narrative necklace. Form criticism, from the German word *Formgeschichte,* attempts to unstring the pearls in order to come to a better understanding of the original saying or event.

The results of such scholarship have been invaluable in helping us understand how the Gospels were constructed and how the tradition was preserved, although many of the conclusions concerning the historicity of the Gospels are far from convincing.

In all these ways we see the obvious relationship of the Gospels to one another. Equally important, however, are the distinguishing characteristics of each. One reason why harmonies of the Gospels are never successful is that the Gospels, though closely related, have been written from very different points of view. Each writer sees his subject from a different perspective, thus adding to the finished portrait of Jesus. For this reason the student of the life of Jesus must know something of the distinguishing characteristics of each of the Gospels.

The Gospel of Mark was probably written by John Mark, a Jewish Christian disciple whose mother's home may have been a place of prayer for the earliest Christians in Jerusalem. He was a missionary companion of Paul and a secretary for Peter. Shortly after the death of Peter in Nero's persecution, Mark wrote the first Gospel, depending primarily upon what he had learned from Peter. Since he was writing for Roman Christians who were facing persecution, he hurries through the early ministry in order to emphasize the suffering and death of Jesus in a tense dramatic account of the ministry in Jerusalem. Some of the distinguishing characteristics of the book of Mark are as follows: (1) It is the briefest Gospel. (2) It contains the greatest detail of everyday life in Palestine. (3) It is the most dramatic of the Gospels. (4) It is the most unpolished in literary form. (5) It emphasizes the life more than the teaching of Jesus, the narrative rather than the sayings.

The Gospel of Matthew was placed first in the New Testament probably because the early church recognized its excellence of arrangement for reading and instruction. Most scholars agree that the author is unknown, although a collection of material by the apostle Matthew may be the nucleus around which the finished

work was collected. It was probably written around the year
A.D. 85 in the city of Antioch where there was a strong early
church. His clear dignified style falls somewhere between Mark's
ruggedness and Luke's literary artistry. Some distinguishing characteristics of Matthew: (1) He is interested in the Old Testament, especially the Messianic prophecies that he believes are fulfilled in Jesus. (2) He is more interested in the church than any
other Gospel writer. This ecclesiastical interest partly accounts
for his special attention to Peter, the leader of the early church.
(3) He has a greater interest in the teaching of Jesus, devoting
three fifths of his Gospel to the sayings or words of Jesus. (4) He
arranges the teaching material into five long discourses. (5) Only
Matthew contains the Sermon on the Mount.

The Gospel of Luke begins with a formal preface and was intended as the first volume of a larger work on the history of
Christianity. It was written by Luke, the beloved physician and
companion of Paul. His style betrays his Greek background and
demonstrates his unusual literary and historical ability. It was
probably written around the year A.D. 80 and is often associated
with the city of Corinth, one of the strong but restless churches
founded by Paul. Distinguishing characteristics of the book of
Luke: (1) It is more artistic and polished in style. (2) It is the
only Gospel written by a Gentile. (3) Luke is especially interested
in the poor, in sinners, and in the welfare of women. (4) He is
especially interested in the prayer life of Jesus. (5) He records
more parables than does any other Gospel, many of them in his
unique "travel document" (Luke 9:51 to 18:43), which describes the journey of Jesus to Jerusalem.

Having surveyed the two preliminary questions, the world of
Jesus and the available sources, we are now well prepared to in-
vestigate his life and teaching. In doing so, it is necessary for us
to realize that the life and teaching can never be separated in
actual practice, for the teaching grew out of the life and the life

demonstrated the teaching. For purposes of study, however, it is convenient to divide them, beginning with the life or ministry and later interpreting the teaching or message in detail. Who was Jesus? What did he say? These are the two crucial questions for Christian theology and Christian experience.

THE LIFE OF JESUS

3

Early Life

THE STORY of Jesus begins under the light of a bright star. According to Matthew, the star guided Wise Men from the East to Bethlehem, the city of David, where they found and worshiped an infant who had been born king of the Jews. According to Luke, humble shepherds also came, having felt the glory of the Lord and having heard the singing of angels. Matthew and Luke tell the story with superb literary artistry, both accounts throbbing with the joy of fulfilled expectation.

A. GENEALOGY

Ancestry was an important matter to the Jewish people, especially in the case of anyone who made Messianic claims, for it was common knowledge that the Messiah would be a descendant of David, the greatest of Israel's kings. Matthew and Luke therefore include genealogical tables to show the Davidic ancestry of Jesus. (Matt. 1:1-17; Luke 3:23-38.) Matthew continues back to Abraham, the first Hebrew. Luke betrays his Gentile background by continuing all the way back to Adam, the first man. The main purpose of these genealogies is quite clear, but one or two related problems are not so easily explained.

The first problem arises when the two tables are compared, for they agree on only a very few names. Between Joseph and David, for example, they coincide only three times. Matthew, moreover, includes five women in his genealogy, a practice highly unusual among the Hebrews. There are three main theories usually proposed to explain the discrepancy: (1) Some have maintained that Matthew gives us the genealogy of Joseph, whereas Luke gives that of Mary. (2) Others have held that Matthew gives the legal descent, whereas Luke gives his physical or natural descent. (3) Since neither of these theories rests on any historical evidence, most scholars simply assume that there were at least two separate traditions concerning the ancestry of Jesus. Matthew and Luke have each given us one of the traditions, having found them in their own special sources.

The real problem of the genealogies, however, arises when they are matched against the story of the virgin birth. Only Matthew and Luke state that Jesus was born of a virgin, yet both of these authors include genealogies tracing the ancestry of Jesus through Joseph. If Joseph was not his real father, then the family trees are invalid, since their purpose is to show that Jesus was of Davidic blood. Matthew and Luke or some later editors were aware of the difficulty because the text shows signs of editing. Matthew suddenly diverts the ancestral line from Joseph to Mary: " Jacob the father of Joseph the husband of Mary, of whom Jesus was born." Luke solves the problem with a parenthetical comment: " Jesus, when he began his ministry, was about thirty years of age, being the son (as was supposed) of Joseph." These editorial corrections do not solve the problem, however, for the real purpose of the genealogies is to show that Jesus is a descendant of David *through Joseph*.

Actually, therefore, the tables are of much greater symbolical than historical value. At the time when the Gospels were written it was believed that Jesus was a " son of David," thus fulfilling Old Testament prophecy and Jewish belief about the Messiah. Matthew and Luke, by including a genealogical table near the beginning of their Gospels, demonstrate their awareness of this common belief about Jesus. Having once made the point, however, they do not return to it. Finally, it should be pointed out that Jesus made no point of his Davidic ancestry, nor did he ever use the material in these tables to support the authority of his Messianic claim.

B. BIRTH

Like their genealogies, the matchless infancy narratives of Matthew and Luke obviously come from separate traditions. (Matt. 1:18 to 2:23; Luke 1:1 to 2:40.) The popular mind has merged the descriptions into one "Christmas story," but each follows a very different order of events.

According to Matthew, the story begins with a dream. Joseph, deeply troubled by Mary's expectant condition, is assured in a dream that the child has been conceived of the Holy Spirit: " She will bear a son, and you shall call his name Jesus, for he will save his people from their sins." Matthew apparently knew nothing of the long trip from Nazareth to Bethlehem or of the birth in a stable. He tells of the birth in a single sentence and then moves directly into his account of the coming of Wise Men from the East where they had seen the star that meant that a king had been born. Offering their gifts, they returned to their own country, avoiding Herod, who was eager to find out more about this future king. The flight into Egypt, the massacre of the innocent children in Bethlehem, and the journey to set up a new home in Nazareth complete Matthew's infancy narrative. We do not find any record of these last-mentioned events in any other source, yet a ruthless man like Herod who killed his own sons would scarcely hesitate to kill the sons of others if he felt a threat to his throne. The slaughter of children, marring the otherwise joyous note of Jesus' infancy narratives, is symbolic, for the overtones of tragedy in the music of his birth continued throughout his life, even to the cross.

Luke's Christmas story is much longer than Matthew's. He begins with the birth of John the Baptist, the new Elijah preparing the way for the Messiah who would give light to those who sit in darkness and in the shadow of death. The announcement to Mary and Mary's visit to Elizabeth are described in prose and poetry, heightening the sense of expectancy. Then Luke describes the journey from Nazareth to Bethlehem, the crowded inn, and the birth in the stable. He does not waste words, but hastens to describe the visit of the shepherds and Mary's concern as she contemplates the future of her infant son. Following Jewish custom, Joseph and Mary then take Jesus to the Temple, where he is presented to the Lord and redeemed with a gift of money. Here Simeon and Anna have been waiting through the long years for the coming of the Messiah. When Simeon sees Jesus he cries out, "Lord, now lettest thou thy servant depart in peace, . . . for mine eyes have seen thy salvation." Luke has interspersed throughout his infancy narrative exquisite poetry, sensitive prose, and a mood of joyous fulfillment unsurpassed anywhere in the Bible.

Every student of the life of Jesus must decide how much of these infancy stories is fact and how much is legend since there are obvious difficulties in the material as presented by Matthew and Luke. While still a very small boy, Albert Schweitzer asked his parents why Joseph and Mary continued to be so poor if the Wise Men had brought such rich gifts. This and countless similar questions are difficult to answer until we realize that a good deal of the Christmas story is legend. Unfortunately, the word "legend" has often been associated with falsehood, but a legend is simply history as experienced or remembered. A historical fact grows into a legend when the impact of a person's life will not let the minds of those who knew him rest with simple history. There is almost always a kernel of historical fact at the heart of a legend, but the legendary way in which the fact is presented often tells us more about a person than volumes of documented history. The present state of the infancy narratives is thus invaluable in telling us about Jesus and what he meant to others.

A summary of the ten major points in the Christmas story will illustrate how fact and legend have mingled at many different levels. Each reader must decide for himself where fact ends and legend begins, remembering in each case the value of legend as "remembered history."

1. Jesus was born. This is the most obvious fact of all, but there are two good reasons for stating it. In the first place, many persons who believe in Christ describe him in terms that make him seem like some supernatural visitor from another world, utterly unrelated to humanity's pain, sorrow, and suffering. The fact that he was born is significant because it means that he submitted to all the disciplines of growth implied in human birth. In the second place, some scholars in the nineteenth century denied the existence of Jesus, claiming that he was a myth. This view is no longer held by any reputable scholar; hence it is not necessary to enter into a lengthy discussion of the arguments that were advanced. Suffice it to say that we have as much evidence for the existence of Jesus as we have for most of the figures of the ancient world. He was born.

2. He was born in humble surroundings. Many things about the birth suggest this fact: the manger in the stable, Joseph's trade as a carpenter, the poor man's sacrifice that the parents made at the Temple—"a pair of turtledoves, or two young pigeons." Those who believe in the incarnation find it significant that when God chose to visit his people he came in lowly, humble, commonplace surroundings.

3. He was born a Jew. Many modern Christians think of the Jews as the people who killed Jesus. It would be far better to remember them as the people who produced Jesus. The infancy narratives clearly illustrate the importance of the Jewish tradition in the home into which he was born: humble piety, fulfilled prophecy, the law, Messianic expectancy, and worship in the Temple.

4. He was born in Bethlehem. This seems fairly certain, though

discrepancies in the records have led to scholarly debates on this point. According to Matthew, Joseph and Mary lived in Bethlehem. Jesus was born there, at home, and the family then moved to Nazareth only because they wanted to avoid persecution. According to Luke, Joseph and Mary lived in Nazareth and went to Bethlehem in order to comply with the rules of the Roman Government concerning the census. In spite of these difficulties, however, most scholars agree that the birth took place in Bethlehem.

5. He was born around 7 to 4 B.C. It seems absurd to say that he was born B.C. (Before Christ), but the medieval scholar who first determined our present chronological system miscalculated. Since Herod the Great died in 4 B.C., Jesus must have been born before that date. How much before we do not know, but as indicated below, an unusual star appeared in 7 B.C.

6. His birth was accompanied by unusual visitors. Luke says that shepherds came in from the surrounding hill country, while Matthew reports the visit of Wise Men or astrologers from the East. Neither report is unreasonable, though it seems likely that legendary material would quickly grow up around such events. Many persons think of the story of the Wise Men as a work of art in which the author presents Christ as the object of worship for men all over the world.

7. His birth was accompanied by unusual signs. Angels sang and acted as messengers, and a bright star appeared, as if people wanted to say, " This event has cosmic significance." In deciding how much of this material is historical, the reader should know that Jupiter and Saturn were in close conjunction three times in 7 B.C. and that Halley's comet passed over the area in 12 B.C. Whether historical or not, however, such details are included to show that the birth of Jesus was no ordinary event.

8. His birth caused Herod to slaughter the male children of Bethlehem. There is no record of this massacre in any other historical source, hence some believe it is a legend. On the other

hand, Herod was ruthless and reacted violently against any threat to his imperial security.

9. The family fled to Egypt to escape persecution. If Herod's massacre is historical, this may well be the corollary, though Matthew's brief notice is the only record of the event.

10. Jesus was born of a virgin. This is the most controversial point in the narratives of Jesus' birth. In fact, more heat has been generated in arguments over the virgin birth of Jesus than any other aspect of his life. Some of his followers, supposedly loving one another, have said many unloving things about those who disagree with them on the problem of the virgin birth. Is it fact or legend?

Unfortunately, the question is difficult to answer because the virgin birth cannot be categorically proved or disproved. Every piece of evidence offered to prove it can be matched with equally convincing arguments against it.

On the one hand, it is definitely affirmed in Matt. 1:18-25 and Luke 1:34-35, and the story is never denied in the New Testament. On the other hand, Matthew and Luke refute their own statements by including genealogical tables that trace the descent of Jesus through Joseph. Neither writer ever refers to the matter again, and both include statements in which Jesus is known as "Joseph's son" (Matt. 13:55; Luke 4:22). The story, moreover, is never affirmed at any other point in the New Testament. Mark's silence is troubling, since his was the earliest Gospel. John's silence is troubling, since he was concerned more than the others to show how Jesus was the unique Son of God. Paul's silence is troubling, since Paul was especially interested in the eternal meaning of the life of Jesus and wrote long before the Gospels appeared. On top of all this, Jesus never mentions the matter, nor does he ever make belief in it a condition for discipleship.

Further, it is often insisted that the virgin birth is foretold in the Old Testament, especially in Isa. 7:14: " Behold, a virgin shall conceive, and bear a son." Actually, however, this idea is nowhere definitely stated in the Old Testament except in this one passage in Isaiah and this passage was obviously not intended as a reference to the virgin birth of the long-expected Messiah. The Hebrew word *almah,* which is used, means "young woman," not "virgin." If Isaiah had wanted to refer to a virgin, he would have used a different word. Moreover, any fair-minded reading of the seventh chapter of Isaiah will make it clear that the author was referring to events in his own time. In typical prophetic fashion, Isaiah was giving King Ahab a sign: by the time a certain young woman had borne a son, the king would see the folly of his trust in political alliances rather than in the strength of the Lord.

Some insist that the possibility of a virgin birth has not been disproved even though it is generally denied by science. Moreover, there have been some reports of virgin births taking place in modern times. On the other hand, science has shown that the offspring of a virgin birth would have to be female due to the absence of male chromosomes. Even if other virgin births did occur, however, they would rob the birth of Jesus of its uniqueness, since the main purpose of the doctrine of the virgin birth is to show that Jesus is unlike every other human being.

Thus the arguments cancel each other out until we realize the impossibility of proving or disproving the virgin birth of Jesus on the grounds of historical evidence. The issue is finally decided on the basis of personal religious experience. What we believe about Jesus and what we have known about him determine what we believe about the virgin birth. In general, Christian experience has led in three directions.

According to one view, Jesus must be qualitatively different from other men if he is truly the Son of God. He must be free from the weaknesses and limitations of humanity and he must be free from the sinfulness inherent in natural conception and human birth. Thus he was born miraculously of a virgin in order to establish his uniqueness as the Son of God.

According to a second view, Jesus must not be qualitatively different from other men if he is truly a Savior. How could ordinary men hope to follow him if he is essentially different in the way implied by a virgin birth? As one protested, "A virgin birth for Jesus would set him apart from the rest of humanity, so that his challenge would be unfair." It would also destroy the real meaning of some of the major events in his life. The supernatural quality implied in a virgin birth, for example, makes the agony of the temptation and Gethsemane quite meaningless. On the other hand, if he continuously faced real decision, growing in full acceptance of the will of God, then he is truly a Savior.

According to the third view, we cannot know the answer to this problem, nor is it especially important. Since Jesus does not mention his virgin birth, nor make it a condition for following him, the true essence of the Christian life lies elsewhere. This Christian agnosticism on the matter of the virgin birth is a widely held view among modern followers of Jesus.

One final word of warning is in order. Many Protestants confuse the virgin birth and the Immaculate Conception. As we have just seen, the virgin birth refers to Jesus and is an elective matter of faith in Protestantism. The Immaculate Conception, on the other hand, is a Roman Catholic dogma referring to Mary. It states that at the moment of her conception a miracle took place, removing all taint of original sin. Since Mary thus lived a sinless life, she ascended bodily to heaven. The virgin birth, the Immaculate Conception of Mary, and the bodily Assumption of Mary are all dogmas of the Roman Church, which means they must be accepted without question. The latter two should never be confused with the virgin birth, which alone is mentioned in Scripture.

Before closing this survey of the birth of Jesus, a word should be said about the Christian belief in the incarnation. "Incarnation" comes from a Latin word meaning "flesh," or more specifically "enfleshment," the act of taking on flesh or human form. The word is used by Christians to describe their conviction that the eternal God took on human form in the person of Jesus. There are differing ways of explaining the incarnation, some emphasizing the virgin birth, others looking more to the unique filial consciousness of Jesus. But whatever the explanation, the incarnation itself is one of the fundamental beliefs of Christendom. In some way the holy God "became flesh and dwelt among us." As a loving Father he comes to us. This experience is nowhere expressed more beautifully than in the joy, the light, and the music of the Christmas story in the Gospels.

C. YOUTH

Unfortunately, except for one brief notice in Luke, there is no record of the youth of Jesus. These "hidden years" have been almost entirely obscured by the passing of time. Luke tells us that "the child grew and became strong, filled with wisdom; and the favor of God was upon him" (Luke 2:40). Modern biographers, dissatisfied with this short notice, have tried to fill in details by reading back into his childhood what he was in adult life and by assuming that he was a normal member of his social environment. Using this method of historical speculation, we may sketch in the rough outlines of his youthful development.

His home life was apparently humble and wholesome. In the home, Jesus would receive the fundamentals of an education and he would be taught his father's trade. According to the Gospels, he had brothers and sisters. As the eldest son he may have assumed responsibility for the family when Joseph died. Religion was undoubtedly at the center of his life. His education and his Sabbath worship would be based on the Jewish Law and Prophets. He would be caught up in the Messianic expectancy of his people and would look forward to the coming of God's Kingdom.

His education would continue in the synagogue school when he reached a certain age. Here the children would sit and repeat the passages of Scripture that the rabbi read and explained to them. His cultural environment was not as limited as is often supposed, for important caravan routes ran close to Nazareth. Finally, we may assume that he spent much of his time out of doors, for in later life he demonstrated an unusual knowledge and love of nature.

The only glimpse of Jesus' youth afforded by the Gospels occurs when he is twelve years old. (Luke 2:41-52.) At that age a Jewish boy would be admitted to the status of " Son of the Law " (Ben-Torah). At this time he became a man, responsible for himself in the sight of the law. When Jesus was twelve his parents took him to Jerusalem for this ceremony.

In popular fancy, Jesus has been pictured in the Temple, examining the wise teachers in order to confound them. It is more probable that he simply welcomed this opportunity to learn from them. Doubtless he had found that many of his questions could not be answered by his teacher in the synagogue school at Nazareth. Keenly intelligent, deeply interested in the faith of his people, Jesus brought all of his unanswered questions to those who should be able to answer. More than anything else, the incident illustrates his eagerness, even as a young man, to grow in the knowledge of God. The answer that he gave his parents further emphasizes this eagerness: " Did you not know that I must be in my Father's house? " No wonder his mother " kept all these things in her heart."

After this, Luke tells us that Jesus went back to Nazareth and lived in obedience to his parents. He " increased in wisdom and in stature, and in favor with God and man," but beyond this we know nothing. The curtain closes around him and when he appears again he has reached his full maturity, ready to find and fulfill his divine vocation.

4

Galilean Ministry

ACCORDING to the Synoptic Gospels, the public ministry of Jesus falls into three main periods. It began in Galilee where he enjoyed great popularity at first but soon ran into serious opposition that caused him to journey to Jerusalem. The leisurely journey and the events that occurred along the way constitute the second phase of his ministry. The last days are then spent in what is usually called the Judean ministry. By placing the birth and youth at the beginning of this public ministry and the crucifixion and resurrection at the end, a simple outline is obtained that is very helpful in remembering the movement of his life as a whole.

The general nature of the ministry in Galilee is quite clear. It was essentially a wandering or itinerant ministry whose theme was the Kingdom (reign or rule) of God. He seemed to make Capernaum a kind of headquarters, but he never stayed in any one place very long. Whereas John the Baptist had preached in the wilderness, letting the people come to him, Jesus went out to the people. The incidents reported in the Gospels take place in various scenes, sometimes in the house at Capernaum, sometimes on the shore of the lake or in a boat, sometimes on a hillside or in the country, occasionally in a synagogue. Most of the time he was either teaching or healing. He was greeted by a wave of popular enthusiasm at first: " 'What is this? A new teaching!

With authority he commands even the unclean spirits, and they obey him.' And at once his fame spread everywhere throughout all the surrounding region of Galilee." (Mark 1:27-28.) But he soon ran into serious opposition from the Pharisees and Herodians, so that he was forced to change his strategy, ending the Galilean ministry and heading toward Jerusalem.

The theme of the Galilean ministry is the reign or rule of God, translated in our English versions of the Bible as "Kingdom." This translation is unfortunate, since the word "kingdom" ordinarily connotes a realm or sphere including a king and his subjects. This is only part of what Jesus means when he uses the expression, his main emphasis falling upon the ruling or reigning activity of God over individuals and society. We shall examine the concept of God's reign more carefully when we look at the teaching of Jesus. It is enough at this point to emphasize this as the central theme of his life and ministry. Even the healing incidents are viewed simply as signs that the reign of God is near. Jesus talks about many aspects of his subject, but his theme is always the same.

When Martin Niemoeller visited the United States after the Second World War, he was followed by a group of reporters who expected him to talk about his harrowing experiences in a concentration camp or about conditions in postwar Germany. One by one the reporters left him, however, one of them unknowingly paying him a compliment by saying disgustedly, "All that man talks about is Jesus Christ!" Looking back over the ministry of Jesus, one could say, "All that man talks about is the reign of God!" It is the theme of all his teaching, from his first public sermon to his last private counsel with the disciples. This was his message: "The time is fulfilled, and the kingdom of God is at hand."

A. Baptism and Temptation

The prelude to the Galilean ministry occurred on the banks of
the Jordan and in the wilderness. (Mark 1:1-8.) Jesus had journeyed down to the river to hear his cousin John preaching and
there he submitted to the baptism of John. During this experience
he received the call from God to his Messianic vocation, after
which he spent time in the wilderness, searching for the meaning
of the experience and for the direction of his future calling.

John the Baptist, who performed the rite of baptism, was a stern
and austere prophet, living out in the wilderness in rough clothes
and existing on an ascetic diet. His wilderness preaching attracted large crowds, who came from great distances to hear him,
even though his messages were violent and disturbing. He was
a man of fearless courage, calling the leading Pharisees " a brood
of vipers," and reproving King Herod for his immorality. Herod
imprisoned John in a fortress on the shores of the Dead Sea, there
putting him to death. Josephus, the Jewish historian, says that
John was killed because of the danger of a potential revolution.
Mark says that he was killed after Salome's famous dance because
he had dared rebuke Herod and his queen.

John's preaching was powerful and effective in its presentation
of judgment and repentance. His metaphors of judgment were
unforgettable: vipers fleeing the flames of a burning field, wind
separating the chaff from the wheat and fire consuming it, the
woodman's ax lying ready at the foot of the tree. In view of this
imminent judgment, John urged men to repent and escape from
the wrath to come. He required a new start in men's lives, sym-
bolized by the act of repentance and baptism for past sins. John
was weak in applying his message to specific ethical situations,
but his pictures of judgment and his exhortations to repentance
are unsurpassed in the history of prophetic preaching.

John's true greatness, however, lies in his role as the forerunner
of Jesus. The Gospels emphasize this by quoting Old Testament

passages about the one who was coming to prepare the way of the Lord. John accepted this role, speaking of one " who is mightier than I, the thong of whose sandals I am not worthy to stoop down and untie." One old painting of John has captured this aspect of his life magnificently. In the painting, John stands pointing toward Jesus as if he is saying, " Behold! " The artist has so centered attention on John's pointing finger that it seems to dominate the picture. The total impression of the painting is made by John's finger pointing away from himself toward Jesus. This is his major role in the Gospel drama, preparing the way for Jesus by setting the stage and performing the initial act of baptism.

The baptism was undoubtedly one of the crucial events in the life of Jesus. (Mark 1:9-11 and parallels.) All the Synoptics agree in describing Jesus' presentation of himself to John at the Jordan. According to Matthew, John protested briefly, but consented upon the insistence of Jesus. The exact form of John's baptismal rite is unknown, although it probably consisted of pouring or immersion. Many commentators believe that the convert immersed himself in the Jordan as John directed from the bank. When Jesus came up out of the water he felt the presence of God in an intensely vivid experience that he interpreted as God's call to a unique vocation: " Thou art my beloved Son; with thee I am well pleased."

Since John submitted his converts to a baptism for the forgiveness of sins, Christians face the problem of deciding why Jesus was baptized. Many enemies of the early church insisted that Jesus must have been conscious of sin. The disciples of John, moreover, insisted that their master was superior to Jesus since Jesus had been baptized by John. In view of these difficulties, Christian scholars have suggested many reasons for the baptism of Jesus. The following suggestions have been made at various stages in the history of Christian thought. (1) Jesus was baptized in order to elicit a Messianic response from John or as a sign to

John. (2) He was baptized as an anointing, as king of the new Kingdom. (3) He was baptized as a declaration of his intention to enter into his public ministry. (4) He was baptized in order to identify himself with his sinful and repentant people. (5) He was baptized as an example, not because he needed it, but because others do. (6) He was baptized as a sign of the identification of himself with the general movement preached by John, especially as it related to the expected reign of God. In many ways this seems to be the most reasonable answer and is probably what is intended in the brief passage in Matthew when Jesus insists that John baptize him: " Let it be so now; for thus it is fitting for us to fulfil all righteousness " (Matt. 3:15). This may mean "to fulfill all righteous acts, thus fulfilling all conditions for the Kingdom." Later Jesus departs from John's conception of the Kingdom, but here he may be identifying himself with that which was to become the theme of his own life and ministry.

What actually happened to Jesus at the time of his baptism? This is a difficult question to answer in view of the confusion in the records. According to Mark, the Voice, the dove, the open heavens are experienced by Jesus alone. In Matthew, however, the Voice speaks to the people rather than to Jesus. In Luke, on the other hand, the Voice speaks directly to Jesus, but the dove descends in bodily form for all to see. Here is an outstanding example of the way in which the later followers of Jesus transformed an inner spiritual experience into an outward miraculous event. The fact that this was an inner experience of Jesus and not an outward miracle fits well with all that happened afterward. Neither John nor the disciples act as if they had a sign from heaven confirming Jesus as the Messiah. John, in fact, later sends messengers to ask Jesus, " Are you he who is to come, or shall we look for another? " (Matt. 11:3.) This question, from Q, thus confirms Mark's opinion that the real meaning of the baptism is found in what it meant to Jesus.

From the event in the Temple at the age of twelve and from

events in his later life, it is safe to assume that Jesus throughout life had a growing awareness of his unique filial relationship to God. This unique filial relationship manifested itself in an increasing God-consciousness and in an awareness of his Messianic vocation. It is impossible for us to know how far these had developed prior to his baptism, but it is certain that in the intense experience of God that occurred at the baptism he received a vivid confirmation of his unique relationship to God. This was a moment of direct revelation, a deep mystical awareness of the living presence of God. It was at the same time a moment in which Jesus experienced with new intensity God's call to his Messianic vocation. Later, Jesus may have told the disciples about what had happened, perhaps describing the feeling of God's Spirit entering his consciousness gently, " like a dove," thus using a familiar metaphor to suggest the Spirit's creative, life-giving power.

Following the baptismal experience, Jesus felt the need to be alone to make important decisions concerning his future. (Matt. 4:1-11.) The Gospels describe the forty days in the wilderness as a time of trial when he was tempted to misuse the power that he derived from his unique consciousness of God's presence. There was also the problem of defining his Messianic role, for there were many ideas about the Messiah in current use. One by one the temptations came.

The first temptation, turning stones into bread, was the temptation to become an economic Messiah. Moved by the physical needs of the " people of the land," Jesus was tempted to use the Messianic office as a means of securing economic relief. The temptation to become an economic Messiah must have sorely tried him, for as a man of compassion he had felt deeply the hunger and need of his people. History, moreover, has demonstrated the danger of hunger in fomenting political revolution. But Jesus knew that man does not live by bread alone. Individual and social life ultimately collapse when based on the outward aspects of existence. Jesus rejected the first temptation.

The second temptation, jumping off the pinnacle of the Temple, was the temptation to use his power for his own personal gain, becoming a miracle worker to impress the crowds. Many persons expected the Messiah to be a hero on the grand scale, dazzling his followers with miraculous feats and stunning his enemies into awed submission. But Jesus knew that miracle-mongering is only temporarily effective, furnishing no permanent basis for a religious movement. The Messianic call was no call to become a supernatural magician! Jesus rejected the second temptation.

The third temptation, using evil means to conquer the kingdoms of the world, was the temptation to become a political and military Messiah. This was probably the greatest of all, for this is what most of the people expected. Living in a tense political atmosphere, galled by the iron yoke of Rome, the people eagerly anticipated the coming of a great military and political hero who would destroy the enemies of Israel and establish the Kingdom of God with its center on Mount Zion. The country was teeming with Zealots, as we have seen, anxious to use violence and military power to hasten the revolution. But Jesus knew that he could not use evil means to achieve God's end. He could not use the devil's methods to do God's work. Any religious movement based on physical force would ultimately fail. Jesus rejected the third temptation.

It would be difficult to overemphasize the strength of these temptations for a man of compassion and God-consciousness living in a world of economic need that was teeming with political unrest. It is no wonder that the Gospels have recorded the experience in such vivid allegorical terms, terms that Jesus himself may have used in telling the disciples about it at a later date. Perhaps he told them after the experience in Caesarea Philippi when the temptations came anew. Like the baptism, however, the core of meaning in the temptation is in the inner experience of Jesus.

Here he rejects the ways of man and accepts the way of God.

The type of Messianic vocation that Jesus chose in the wilderness becomes clear as his ministry unfolds. One thing he must have known from the beginning. His decision would not be popular among a people who had very definite ideas of their own. He apparently chose to suffer, if necessary, to call men to a life of holy obedience to God's rule, but he would meet strong opposition from a people who had their hearts set on bread, miracles, and political freedom. The attempt to change their basic ideas about God's rule and the Messiah would probably involve suffering, sacrifice, and perhaps even death. It seems likely that the temptations recurred again and again in his ministry as the crowd tried to make him a king, as his friends constantly misunderstood him, and as his enemies plotted to kill him. But Jesus never faltered in following the decision that he had made alone with God in the wilderness.

B. JESUS AS TEACHER AND PREACHER

When he heard that John the Baptist had been arrested, Jesus began the active phase of his Galilean ministry with a sermon. Mark has recorded the event in two of the most important verses in the New Testament: "Now after John was arrested, Jesus came into Galilee, preaching the gospel of God, and saying, 'The time is fulfilled, and the kingdom of God is at hand; repent, and believe in the gospel.'" (Mark 1:14-15.) From this time on, Jesus looked upon proclaiming and explaining the good news of God's reign as his central task. He traveled widely throughout Galilee, preaching and teaching men about the reign of God. Sometimes he taught directly, sometimes by example, sometimes in unforgettable word pictures. As his ministry developed, his life itself became the outstanding example of his teaching. He even looked upon the healing ministry that took so much of his time as a secondary function. The healing miracles were simply signs of the Kingdom's imminence.

The common people flocked to hear Jesus because he taught as one who had authority and not as the scribes who parroted others. He spoke of the reign of God as if it was the most important thing in life — the pearl of great price and the treasure hidden in the field. He talked about it out of his own personal experience and he talked about it with a note of urgency unknown among other teachers. The reign of God was an immediate possibility. It was at hand! No wonder there was so much excitement wherever he went.

He also emphasized the fact that the Kingdom was the gift of God. Nothing that man could do would hasten or impede the coming of God's rule. The matter was in God's hands and it was his " good pleasure " to give us the Kingdom. It was a free gift, available to all who would accept it through the act of repentance and faith. This was the gospel, the good news, and this was another reason why the words of Jesus were welcomed with such enthusiasm and joy.

The teaching of Jesus will be examined more carefully in the second half of this book. It is sufficient now, as we build a coherent picture of his life, to realize that the Galilean ministry is largely a ministry of preaching and teaching. Wherever people would listen, in large crowds or small, he would tell them about the good news of God's reign. He told them of a God whose infinite love was limitless (even the sparrow's fall is known!), relentless (searching till the lost sheep is found), and forgiving (he runs to greet the returning son). He told them that the meaning of life is found in loving obedience to this loving God (seek first God's reign and his righteousness). He told them that when they had been reconciled to this God through repentance and faith they would begin to live a new life. In this new life they would love others in a new way and find all of life charged with a new creative meaning. Thus Jesus, the teacher, fed the hungry hearts of those who heard him in amazement and in gladness.

C. JESUS AS HEALER AND MIRACLE WORKER

The role of Jesus as healer and miracle worker is often emphasized in popular thought to such a high degree that it threatens
to distort the picture of his life and teaching. It is not surprising
that his unusual power attracted wide attention from the beginning, as we see in Mark's Gospel where nearly one third of the
material is devoted to the miracles. Many people today think of
Jesus as a kind of supernatural magician, waving a magic wand
and performing wonders to astound the crowds. It is important,
therefore, to emphasize again that the ministry of Jesus is first
and foremost a ministry of preaching and teaching. He vigorously condemned those who came primarily looking for miracles
and he left a region whenever his healing ministry threatened to
overshadow his efforts to teach. Since his main purpose was to
announce, explain, and illustrate the reign of God, he simply
looked upon the miracles as signs that the reign of God was near.
A good deal of confusion could be avoided if the followers of
Jesus would keep the miracles in proper perspective.

Even more confusion could be avoided, also, if we had a full
appreciation of the difference in attitude between the first century
and the twentieth century on the whole problem of miracles. We
don't even use the word " miracle " to mean the same thing! In
the first century a miracle was interpreted as an act of direct
intervention by God in the natural world. Life moved along in a
fairly regular and trustworthy way when suddenly God " reached
in " to heal a person or cause some marvelous event to take place.
This meant that God upset the regular course of things in ways
that led to unexpected and unpredictable results. In the twentieth
century we no longer look upon miracles as interventions from
outside the natural world, for those who believe in the creative
power of God know that he is active and present everywhere in
his universe. Any event that happens in the natural world is no
less God's act than any so-called miracle. God is using the natural

laws that he has established everywhere and without ceasing. Occasionally he uses those laws in ways that seem marvelous or " miraculous " to us, but such events are no more intervention from " outside " than any of the events that we have come to understand. As man grows in his understanding of the world of nature, more events formerly regarded as miraculous will be " explained," even though they are still wonderful signs of the power of God. Great Christian thinkers very early began to accept this meaningful definition of miracle. Augustine once said, " Miracles are not contrary to nature, but only contrary to what we know about nature."

This different understanding of the nature of miracles also leads to a sharp contrast in the general acceptance of miracles. The first century was a miracle-loving age. One of the most helpful ways to approach the miracles is to read them in their first-century context when miracles were common and universally accepted. The more we come to understand the attitude of the age, the more we realize how restrained and respectable the miracles of Jesus seem in contrast. Countless persons in the first century were performing marvelous events of many kinds, and no religious leader could expect any kind of following if he couldn't perform miracles to substantiate his claims. The Gospel miracles are not isolated phenomena, but are part of the general mood of the times. It certainly isn't strange that we have miracles reported in the Gospels. The wonder is that we don't have more.

In sharp contrast to the miracle-loving attitude of the first century is the scientific attitude of the twentieth century. In the first glow of achievement that came from the incredible advance of modern research and technology, science declared war on religion and religion fought back in a holy crusade. Fortunately for both sides the war is over. Recently there has been increasing co-operation on the frontiers of religious faith and scientific knowledge. Few scientists today would deny the possibility of miracles. They have run into too much unpredictable, unexplained energy in the vastnesses of outer space and in the heart of the atom. Many scientists have become deeply humble in the face of these unpredictables and in this sense at least are among the most deeply religious men of our age.

At the same time modern science has taught us to search relentlessly for greater understanding of those events which we call miraculous. The fact that such events defy explanation at any given time in history does not mean that there is no explanation. Many events that seemed miraculous in the first century are commonplace today. Many events that are miraculous today will be commonplace tomorrow, as science continues to discover the secrets of God's orderly ways. This means that we will search for the historical core of every miracle story and subject it to every known test of truth after we have seen it in its original setting. The truly religious man will enter joyfully into such a search for greater understanding, knowing that increased understanding of the truth leads inevitably to a better knowledge of God and of his purposes for man.

Also essential in any approach to the miracles is a full appreciation of the attitude of Jesus. Here two very important points are all too often overlooked: (1) Jesus condemned in no uncertain terms any faith that rested on miracles. (2) Jesus looked upon the miracles as signs of the imminence of the reign of God.

The first point is so obvious it is difficult to see how anyone can demand a naïve acceptance of miracles as an essential element in the Christian faith. In the wilderness Jesus rejected the temptation to build his Messianic ministry on wonderful acts. He declared later that it was an evil and adulterous generation that seeks after a sign. Any generation that demands wonders as the basis for its religious faith is unfaithful to God. (Matt. 12:39.) He pointed to the Ninevites who were won by Jonah's prophetic preaching and not by miracles, and he pointed to the Queen of Sheba who was awed by Solomon's wisdom and not by miracles. Then he declared that in him his generation possessed one who was greater than Jonah or Solomon. He asserted that if men would not hear Moses and the prophets, neither would they be persuaded if someone should rise from the dead. (Luke 16:31.) Jesus never demanded that a person believe in miracles in order to believe in him. On the contrary, he condemned any such faith in no uncertain terms.

He did, however, look upon the wonderful acts that he was able to perform as signs that the reign of God was near. When John the Baptist was in prison he sent messengers to ask Jesus if he was the Messiah, the one who would initiate the reign of God. Jesus replied by telling the messengers to return to John and tell him how they had seen the lame walk and the blind receive their sight. This would be evidence enough. (Luke 7:18-23.) Later, in the Beelzebul controversy, when he was accused of being able to cast out demons because he was in league with the chief of demons, he replied, " If it is by the finger [power] of God that I cast out demons, then the kingdom of God has come upon you " (Matt. 12:28). In these and other ways Jesus related the miracles to the dominant theme of his life.

In the twentieth century as in the first century, an enlightened approach to the miracles results in a heightened appreciation of Jesus. We now understand better than before what may have happened in the events that the Gospels report as miracles. This is especially true of the healing miracles, for modern medicine has made tremendous strides in healing. But the more we learn, the more astounded we become at the compassion and God-consciousness of Jesus that made it possible for him to do these " marvelous " things. His own deep and unique filial relationship to God apparently made it possible for him to understand the ways of nature and to use natural laws in strange and wondrous ways. This same relationship to God coupled with the deepest compassion and insight into the nature of human personality made it possible for him to heal diseased minds and bodies wherever he went. He was so fully in accord with the will of God that he was able to use God's power in ways that his contemporaries could not explain and in ways that twenty centuries later we still cannot explain. Our faith does not rest upon miracles, but our faith is strengthened by our awareness of Jesus' amazing power made possible through his unique relationship to God.

The interpretation of the reported miracles of Jesus is simplified by dividing them into three general categories: healing miracles, nature miracles, and resuscitations. Most of the miracles fall into the first category. There are only four or five nature miracles and only three instances of raising the dead (resuscitation). It will be impossible within the scope of this book to examine the miracles in detail, but certain helpful observations may be made about these three main categories.

Our appreciation of the healing miracles has increased tremendously with the new insights furnished by modern medicine. There has been an unprecedented curiosity in recent years about faith healing and a growing realization on the part of clergymen and doctors that faith, or at least mental outlook, is a vital element in the process of healing. As we venture into this field with growing enthusiasm the following conclusions already seem assured: (1) The very intimate relationship between mind and body has been established, opening up the whole new field of psychosomatic medicine. Mental illness can lead to physical disease of many kinds, such as ulcers, asthma, blindness, skin disease, tuberculosis, and paralysis. To the uninitiated the close causal relationship seems incredible. For example, a young man who became blind for no apparent organic reason was assured that surgery would restore his sight. An anesthetic was administered and a few harmless scratches were made on his lids. When the bandages were removed a few days later, he could see, and continuing psychotherapy completed the healing process. Countless similar illustrations could be used to show the intimate relationship of mind and body that is now an axiom of medical science. (2) Faith is an essential element in healing. By faith we do not mean intellectual belief, but trust or confidence in some person or power. Ordinarily, trust in God is implied in the process of faith healing, but faith may also involve trust in a physical object (rosary, relic), a place (Lourdes), an act (anointing, laying on of hands), or a person (minister or doctor). Where faith or trust of this kind is missing, healing is impossible as we see in those instances when Jesus was unable to heal among his own people. (3) Faith healing in which there is a sudden and radical cure is very rare but very real. Less than 1 per cent of the pilgrims to Lourdes are healed, but these are examined and their cases verified by competent doctors and other observers. In every generation since Jesus shared the power to heal with his disciples there have been authenticated cases of healing through faith.

A careful reading of the healing miracles in the Gospels makes it clear that Jesus had insight into the nature of healing that modern medicine has yet to attain. His growing consciousness and knowledge of the power of God together with his deep compassion made it possible for him to call forth the faith necessary for healing. He never claimed the healing power for himself, but said simply, "Your faith has made you well." He was able to relate himself to persons in such a creative way that they gained the trust and confidence necessary for the healing powers of God to bring new life and health. Thus in such typical cases as the demoniac of Geresa (Mark 5:1-20), the paralytic who was let down through the roof (ch. 2:1-12), the epileptic boy (ch. 9:14-29), and blind Bartimaeus (ch. 10:46-52) we see the power of Jesus acting to call forth creative, expectant trust. He was able to make faith in God real to others because God was real to him. Modern attempts at faith healing will be successful only as they look to Jesus and learn the life-creating faith that was at the heart of his own ministry of healing.

The nature miracles, though few in number, create certain unusual difficulties. The tendency for a simple historical event to grow into legendary proportions was perfectly natural among miracle-loving people who had been awed by the personality of Jesus. The difficulty comes when we try to separate fact from legend and when we try to determine just what the Gospel writers are trying to say in telling the story as they have. In each of the stories there is probably a perfectly rational historical core. For example, there is a good deal of evidence in the wording and context of the " storm at sea " narrative to lead us to believe that the real heart of the story is the quieting of the storm of fear in the hearts of the disciples. In another famous incident there is some reason to believe that Jesus may have been walking *by* the sea rather than *upon* the sea. When he broke the loaves and fishes before the five thousand perhaps his words and example quite naturally led the crowd to share with one another. Each of the nature miracles has more than one possible rational explanation.

Too much preoccupation with such rational solutions is apt to be quite misleading, however, for at least two reasons. In the first place, it may lead us to underestimate the unsurpassed insight into the ways of nature that Jesus possessed because of his unique relationship to God. This relationship undoubtedly enabled him to do things that his contemporaries thought were marvelous and that we also would think marvelous. In the second place, an overemphasis on rational explanations may lead us to miss the real point of these stories. They were told to enhance the authority of Jesus and to impart to others the impression that he had made on those who loved him. " Who then is this, that even wind and sea obey him? " "And they were utterly astounded, for they did not understand about the loaves." It is well to look for the historical core of the nature miracles, but we should never let this blind us to what these stories can tell us about Jesus and the effect he had upon people.

The three reported cases of resuscitation are especially troubling to many modern students of the life of Jesus. The most astounding case of all, the raising of Lazarus after he had been dead for three days (John, ch. 11), is entirely unknown to Matthew, Mark, and Luke. They certainly would have recorded this most amazing of all the miracles if they had known about it. The account of the raising of the widow's son (Luke 7:11-17) is so brief we cannot tell anything about it. In the raising of Jairus' daughter (Mark 5:21-43) an unusual difficulty is raised by the fact that Jesus says, "The child is not dead but sleeping." What did he mean? Perhaps he meant just what he said, but like the early disciples we laugh at him and do not believe him. Scarcely a year goes by without many reported cases of persons who have been pronounced dead suddenly regaining consciousness. Perhaps Jesus who understood so much about life was no stranger to that no man's land between life and death. If he actually brought people back from the dead, however, why don't the Gospels make more of the fact? This is a real puzzle, but once again we should not let such questions divert us from an appreciation of the impact that Jesus must have made upon those who knew him. They did not even find it incredible that he should raise the dead!

The role of Jesus as healer and miracle worker has assumed unduly large proportions in the thought of his followers. It was a vital phase of his ministry, especially at first, but Jesus himself tried to keep this part of his activity in perspective. Men are not saved by miracles. If they do not accept the reign of God as revealed partially in the Law and the Prophets and fully in Jesus himself, "neither will they be convinced if some one should rise from the dead."

D. JESUS AND THE DISCIPLES

Very early in the Galilean ministry, Jesus called certain men to become his disciples. He apparently called them as learners, helpers, and friends. The word "disciple" means "learner," and this is primarily what they were expected to do as they followed Jesus about. If there was to be any continuing element in his ministry, men would have to be taught and prepared for the future. At the same time, however, Jesus looked upon his disciples as assistants, calling them apostles, which means "messengers" or "those sent." The preaching missions that they undertook at the direction of Jesus were more than mere training sessions. They were extensions of the ministry of Jesus. We should not overlook also the values of friendship that Jesus must have derived from the constant companionship of these sturdy Galileans.

Two sets of brothers, Peter and Andrew, James and John, constitute the inner circle. They were all fishermen on the Sea of Galilee before they left their nets to follow Jesus. Many scholars believe they knew Jesus before he called them, perhaps meeting him as they listened to the prophetic preaching of John the Baptist. Matthew was a tax collector, possibly already known to the other disciples since Mark hints that his tax office was near the sea. When Jesus went to eat in Matthew's house he was condemned by the Pharisees for eating with sinners.

The Synoptic Gospels do not disclose the ways in which any of the other individual disciples were called. They do tell us, however, that twelve were chosen out of the larger crowd " to be with him, and to be sent out to preach and have authority to cast out demons " (Mark 3:14-15). Luke tells us that Jesus continued all night in prayer before choosing the Twelve, a fact which indicates that he placed great importance upon the event. The names of the Twelve are listed once each by Mark and Matthew and twice by Luke, including Acts 1:13. The name of Judas Iscariot always appears last, and he is always identified as the one " who betrayed him."

The instructions that Jesus gave before sending the disciples out on their mission emphasized the need for haste and a willingness to suffer. He told them to move rapidly, wasting no time on those who would not listen. Apparently he felt that time was running out and he did not want them spending it planting where there was little prospect of a harvest. He also made quite clear that his followers would have no easy time. They would live without luxuries and suffer much persecution. No man could be his disciple who was unwilling to take up his cross, to deny himself, to drink the cup of suffering. As we are to see, Jesus related the necessity of suffering to the heart of his own Messianic vocation, and those who followed him would have to be prepared to share that suffering.

The disciples played varied but important roles in the unfolding ministry of Jesus. Peter, the self-appointed leader, was strong and impetuous. His brother Andrew was constantly bringing people to Jesus. James and John were the "sons of thunder." Matthew was a tax collector, hated by his fellow Jews. Thomas was the doubter. Another Simon of whom we hear very little was apparently a Zealot. And Judas was a traitor. In the hearts of all these men but the last, Jesus kindled a fire that spread across the world and continues to burn after twenty centuries. No wonder he prayed all night before he chose them!

E. Jesus as Messiah

Early in the Galilean ministry the question of Messiahship arose for those who came into contact with Jesus. The mentally ill (demon possessed) were the first to use Messianic titles in addressing him, but others soon joined them. Jesus did not openly claim to be the Messiah, but he never disclaimed these titles. He came close to declaring his feeling when he preached in the synagogue at Nazareth, reading a Messianic passage from Isaiah and concluding, "Today this scripture has been fulfilled in your hearing." Apparently the disciples began to talk among themselves, for Jesus questioned them: "Who do men say that I am? . . . Who do you say that I am?" From the moment of his baptism, and perhaps even before, he felt himself called to be the Messiah. Others sensed it from the beginning, even though Jesus made no open declaration.

The problem is that he was not the kind of Messiah people expected. There were many current ideas about the Messiah, but for the most part he was expected to be a great warrior-king who would restore the greatness of national power to Israel. Jesus was not this kind of Messiah. His role was to announce the reign or Kingdom of God as a spiritual relationship of reconciliation and holy obedience and to demonstrate with his own life what it meant to live in that Kingdom. It soon became apparent that he would have to suffer to get this message across to men, so he applied the Old Testament concept of the Suffering Servant to himself. The fact that the Messiah would suffer was unheard of in Jewish thought. We will examine the concept of Messiahship in detail later, but now we can see why Jesus did not openly announce his Messianic vocation. Before he could declare himself to be the Messiah he had to teach men a new concept of Messiahship. It is obvious, however, that he was misunderstood from the very beginning by his family, his friends, and the ruling authorities, both political and ecclesiastical.

This misunderstanding and the ensuing conflict of ideas increased as the Galilean ministry developed. Jesus went all over the region alone and with his disciples, teaching, preaching, and healing. At first he was greeted by a tremendous wave of popular enthusiasm. But he ran into increasing conflict with those who completely misinterpreted his intentions and opposed his interpretation of God's purposes for man. They feared his strange power over the crowds, they despised the ways in which he upset the *status quo,* and they simply would not believe the good news he had come to proclaim. They began to lie in wait for him, trying to trap him in his words. The tension increased and the hatred became more severe as the sunny days of the Galilean ministry rapidly gave way to the gathering storm.

5

Crisis and Journey

T HE STORM of criticism and opposition that gathered strength rapidly forced Jesus to end his ministry in Galilee and make a radical change in strategy. When he discovered that his life was endangered by the intense hostility of the Pharisees and Herodians he left Galilee for a short period of retreat in the Gentile country northwest of Palestine. But this was only a temporary solution. He soon returned and entered into a period of crisis that resulted in a major decision to travel southward toward the enemy's strongest center. This journey to Jerusalem, along with the crucial events leading up to it, constitutes the second major phase in the public ministry of Jesus.

A. Conflict and Controversy

It is necessary to understand the nature of the hostility that arose against Jesus since it was the direct cause of his change in plans. We have already seen that the major opposition arose because he was an unexpected kind of Messiah who preached a new interpretation of the reign of God. For centuries the Jews had been dreaming of the " age to come " when God's Messiah would bring history to an end and initiate the reign or Kingdom of God. They knew what kind of Messiah he would be and how the end would come. But Jesus did not fulfill any of their expectations. When he came as a simple teacher from an out-of-

76

the-way village in the north country, they wanted to know how any good thing could come out of Nazareth. When he tried to tell them that the Messiah must suffer, they refused to believe him. " God forbid, Lord! " cried Peter. When he spent his time talking about the love of God and man's need for repentance and a new life, they were sure he had missed the main point. Moreover, he was dangerous, for he stirred up the people and acted as if many of the fine points of the law were of no importance. They very soon decided that such a false teacher would have to be destroyed.

Even his family and friends misunderstood him and caused no end of trouble. When he preached for the first time in Nazareth, the people who had known him as a boy were first amazed and then incensed because he applied Messianic passages to himself and reprimanded them for their lack of perception. (Luke 4:16-30.) He managed to escape when they tried to kill him, but in view of their violent hostility we can appreciate his later poignant remark, " Foxes have holes, and birds of the air have nests; but the Son of man has nowhere to lay his head " (Luke 9:58). On another occasion his friends tried to seize him and lead him away, convinced that he had gone mad. (Mark 3:21.) Later when he tried to explain the nature of his Messiahship to his own disciples they opposed him. Twice on the journey to Jerusalem they argued over their respective places in the coming Kingdom (Mark 9:33 f. and Mark 10:35 f.), thus demonstrating their complete misunderstanding of his central intention. When he warned his followers that his message would bring misunderstanding among friends and division within families, he was speaking out of his own bitter experience.

The real enemies of Jesus, however, came from the ranks of the Pharisees. They have been much maligned in subsequent history, but are to be commended for their religious zeal and for their honest efforts to adapt the law to the conditions of their own time. Unfortunately, their intense interest in the letter of the law led to crass hypocrisy and empty legalism. Jesus called them "whitewashed tombs, which outwardly appear beautiful, but within they are full of dead men's bones and all uncleanness" (Matt. 23:27). He said they were like serpents, a brood of vipers. Such harsh words arose from his concern over the spiritual blindness and insensitivity that led them to oppose the central thrust of his ministry. They were so blind that when Jesus proclaimed the good news of God they charged him with blasphemy!

The specific points of issue between Jesus and the Pharisees are beautifully illustrated in a cycle of five conflict stories that Mark presents early in his Gospel.

1. Conflict over forgiveness of sins. (Mark 2:1-12.) In the case of the paralytic lowered through the roof, Jesus realized that the man's illness was caused by his heavy burden of guilt. He said, therefore, "My son, your sins are forgiven." There were scribes standing nearby, the teachers and interpreters of the law, who resented Jesus' words. Only a priest could officially pronounce the divine forgiveness of sins. "Who is this man," they demanded, "to take upon himself the authority to forgive sin?"

2. Conflict over eating with sinners. (Mark 2:13-17.) After calling Matthew to be his disciple, Jesus went into Matthew's home as a guest. The scribes of the Pharisees then severely criticized him for mingling with those who were ceremonially unclean. Cleanness of heart was the important thing to Jesus, however, as he continued to minister to the "unclean" people of the land.

3. Conflict over fasting. (Mark 2:18-22.) During a season of fasting, Jesus was criticized for not keeping the fast. The hostility undoubtedly increased when he told the Pharisees that this failure to fast was deliberate. Fasting, he tried to tell them, was a part of the old legalism and had no place in the new age. It would be like patching an old cloak with a piece of new cloth, or like putting new wine into old wineskins, which would break with the fermenting wine. His message could not be contained

within the limits of Jewish legalism.

4. Conflict over Sabbath observance: plucking ears of grain. (Mark 2:23-28.) In the first century there were multitudes of written and oral commandments about keeping the Sabbath Day holy and free from labor. A man could walk so far (two hundred cubits) on the Sabbath but another step was traveling. A woman could not wear ribbons, for this would be carrying a burden. When the hungry disciples of Jesus picked grain and rubbed it in their hands they were condemned for harvesting and threshing on the Sabbath. Answering the Pharisees who criticized them, Jesus used King David as an illustration to show how man's need often justified breaking the law. Laws like the Sabbath law had been instituted to serve man's welfare. Since man was no slave of the Sabbath, anything needful for his welfare might be lawfully done on that day. It is easy to understand the fierce hatred that would have been generated by this attitude of Jesus'.

5. Conflict over Sabbath observance: healing. (Mark 3:1-6.) The observance of the Sabbath became a real point of contention, with the Pharisees hounding Jesus, looking for further breaches of the law. Jesus, sensing their hostility, asked them, " Is it lawful on the Sabbath to do good or to do harm, to save life or to kill? " When they did not answer, he answered himself by healing a man with a withered hand. Jesus observed the Sabbath, but he insisted again that human need took precedence over the law.

Following this last incident, the Gospel tells us that the Pharisees began making definite plans to kill him. " The Pharisees went out, and immediately held counsel with the Herodians against him, how to destroy him." (Mark 3:6.) A popular teacher with such dangerous ideas was too much of a threat to the established patterns of faith and practice. Their hearts were hardened, and they could not appreciate the fresh and creative power in the message and mission of Jesus. They had no imagination and what is worse, they had lost the presence of God in the maze

of legalistic minutiae. Allied with the Herodians, they became
dangerous enemies, forcing Jesus to end his Galilean ministry
and ultimately destroying him.

We know very little about the Herodians. They were probably
officials and supporters of Herod Antipas, Tetrarch in Galilee,
who had already executed John the Baptist and would certainly
execute Jesus if he saw any reason to do so. From time to time
Herod heard about the activities of Jesus and wanted to find out
more about him. (Cf. Mark 6:14-16.) The growing popularity of
Jesus coupled with reports that came from the enemies of Jesus
led Herod finally to the point of decision. "Get away from
here," some friendly Pharisees warned Jesus, "for Herod wants
to kill you." (Luke 13:31-33.)

B. Crisis in Galilee

When Jesus first heard of the threats to his life he left Galilee
and spent some time in the Gentile region of Tyre and Sidon. He
soon returned, however, apparently resolved to accelerate the
declaration of his Messianic mission and to make some basic
change in the course of his ministry. The first resolution reached
a climax in Peter's confession at Caesarea Philippi, the second in
the transfiguration.

Up to this time neither Jesus nor the disciples had openly said
that Jesus was the Messiah. But now, as they walked along the
road toward Caesarea Philippi (Mark 8:27-33), Jesus asked them,
"Who do men say that I am?" They reported the speculation
they had overheard: "John the Baptist, Elijah, one of the
prophets." Then Jesus demanded, "But who do you say that I
am?" Peter replied, "You are the Christ."

According to Matthew, Jesus commended Peter for his insight and bestowed a blessing upon him. According to Mark and
Luke, he simply told the disciples to tell no one about him, since
it was not yet time to declare his vocation openly to the crowds
who were certain to misunderstand his intention. Unfortunately,

the disciples misunderstood also, for when Jesus began to instruct them more definitely about the meaning of his life, relating the Old Testament Suffering Servant passages to himself, they refused to believe him. Peter protested: " God forbid, Lord! This shall never happen to you." At this point Jesus reprimanded Peter severely: " Get behind me, Satan! You are a hindrance to me; for you are not on the side of God, but of men." Jesus recognized in Peter's words a return of the wilderness temptation!

Matthew's addition to the text, a typical example of his special interest in Peter, has caused endless controversy. (Matt. 16:17-19.) What did Jesus mean when he said to Peter, " On this rock I will build my church "? Roman Catholics believe that he was building the church on Peter as the first pope. Protestants insist that he was building the church either on Peter's confession, " You are the Christ," or on Peter as a representative man of faith. In either case, the silence of Mark and Luke is extremely troubling, as is the silence of Jesus about his plans for the church. The word " church " is briefly mentioned in only one other place in the Gospels. (Matt. 18:17.) Further difficulty is created by Jesus' promise of the keys of the Kingdom to Peter. Protestants cannot believe that this power is given to Peter alone, for in other places Jesus confers equal authority upon the other apostles (Matt. 18:18; John 20:23). Evidently Jesus is saying that men of faith who confess Jesus as the Christ will be given the authority to order the life of the church.

Difficulties in Matthew's interpolated passage, however, should not be allowed to divert our attention from the significance of this incident. Peter's confession was one of the landmarks in the gradual unveiling of the " Messianic secret " of Jesus, and it led to one of the crucial events in his life, the transfiguration.

About a week after Peter's confession, Jesus took Peter, James, and John to a high mountain, perhaps somewhere on the slopes of Mount Hermon. (Mark 9:2-8.) Luke says he went there in order to pray. Suddenly he was transfigured, assuming a glorified appearance and talking with Moses and Elijah. Peter, in his excitement, suggested that they build three booths, a customary Hebrew method of marking unusual religious events. But a luminous cloud overshadowed them, and a Voice came from heaven, " This is my beloved Son; listen to him." Suddenly, looking around, they " no longer saw any one with them but Jesus only."

The narrative is crowded with meaningful symbolism. Moses and Elijah represent the Law and the Prophets. The luminous cloud is the Shekinah, the ancient symbol of the divine presence. The divine voice is the *bathkol,* literally the voice of God. Some scholars believe that this symbolism suggests a hallucination. It seems far more likely, however, in view of the ethical and religious content of the description, that this was a genuine mystical experience or vision. Such experiences have played a prominent role throughout the history of religion. Paul's vision on the road to Damascus, Constantine's vision of the cross, and Joan of Arc's vision among the apple blossoms all changed the course of history. Such visions are usually brought on by a state of extreme tension caused by fear or doubt or desire. The vision usually ends the tension and leads to some definite act or resolution.

Peter's vision was of this type. In a great moment he had been the first to acknowledge Jesus as the Messiah. Then when Jesus tried to tell him that the Messiah's life would end in repudiation, disgrace, and death, he plunged from the heights of exhilaration to the depths of despair. When Peter expressed his utter disbelief he was called a Satan! For a week he brooded on the impossibility of a suffering, repudiated Messiah, the tension building up in his mind until it reached a breaking point. Then on the high mountain with Jesus he experienced a genuine mystical vision that resolved his dilemma. The transfigured Lord, the testimony of Moses and Elijah (the Law and the Prophets), and the voice of God from the Shekinah resolved Peter's doubt. The one who was about to be rejected by Judaism was God's Messiah!

This experience on the mountain was also one of the crucial events in the life of Jesus, comparable to the baptism and temptation. Troubled by the failure of his Galilean ministry and the growing hostility of the Pharisees and Herodians, he had to make a decision. Should he remain for the showdown in Galilee, retreat, or change his center of operations? Burdened in spirit, he went up on the mountain to seek guidance through direct communion with God. The fact that he felt a direct and growing filial relationship to God did not mean that every specific choice was made for him. He had to exercise his own free will in choosing the way of obedience to the will of God. Hence the agony in the wilderness, on the Mount of Transfiguration, and in Gethsemane. He prayed so intensely on the mountain that he seemed to be transfigured, a not uncommon fact reported of others lost in the deep places of prayer. A friend of Sadhu Sundar Singh, for example, noted a definite " luminosity " about the Sadhu's face as he prayed alone. Thus lost in the deepest communion with God, seeking to know his will in this situation, Jesus wrestled with the alternatives forced upon him by the crisis in Galilee. We know that the answer came to him, for very soon afterward " he set his face to go to Jerusalem."

This, then, was the point of no return. He would not run away from the hostility, but would carry the conflict back into the enemy's camp. In Jerusalem, the City of David and the heart of Judaism, he would declare the good news of the reign of God, ready to suffer and die, if necessary, to make the message live. His problem in some ways was similar to that faced by many military leaders, outnumbered and in danger of imminent attack. Should he surrender or retreat? Jesus rejected both of these alternatives, gathered all of his strength and attacked first, striking at the enemy's center — Jerusalem!

C. The Journey to Jerusalem

Having made the decision, he knew there was now no need for haste. He traveled at a leisurely pace, filling his days with teaching, healing, and calling new followers. Excitement preceded him all along the way, and wonder remained behind in the hearts of those who met him. Everywhere he went there were crowds, and in the crowds there were enemies, trying to gather evidence from the things he said and did. The route he followed took him straight southward to Samaria where he was turned aside, because Jews and Samaritans " have no dealings with one another." Calming the infuriated disciples, he led them across the Jordan into Peraea and journeyed toward the south. Opposite Jericho they recrossed the river and made straight for Jerusalem.

We are especially indebted to Luke for a detailed report of this phase of Jesus' ministry in a long central section (Luke 9:51 to 18:14) often called " the travel document." He makes no use of Mark, deriving most of his material from Q and his own special source. Following Jesus along the road, Luke describes the people he met, the people he healed, the things he said, the places he visited. Most of the material is of high historic value, though the general order of events is sometimes open to question.

As he traveled, Jesus used every opportunity to proclaim and describe the reign of God. We will examine this teaching in detail at a later point, but it is worth noting now the ways in which Jesus made his teaching vivid by relating it to scenes and events along the way. The parable of the Good Samaritan is made unforgettable by the rejection at the border of Samaria. The parable of the lost sheep would come to life as they journeyed through sheep country, the parable of the vineyard as they paused to refresh themselves along the way. The sight of a happy family may well have prompted him to tell the matchless story of the lost son. We do not know the exact context of most of the parables, but the available evidence would lead us to believe that most of them were made all the more memorable by related events.

He made one now famous stop in the home of Martha and Mary. (Luke 10:38-42.) Martha, the elder sister, eager to serve a satisfying meal, was distracted and anxious about all the details. She reprimanded Jesus for keeping Mary from doing her share of the work, but Jesus replied quietly that Mary, interested in the reign of God, had found the one thing needful.

When a lawyer asked him how to obtain eternal life, Jesus stated the two great commandments of love for God and neighbor. When a rich young man asked him the same question, he told the young man to get rid of his money, which was a hindrance to him, and accept the reign of God. But " when he heard this he became sad, for he was very rich." He blessed the children along the way, healed the sick, and patiently prepared the disciples for the heartache and suffering that were just ahead.

As he crossed the Jordan and drew near to Jericho, blind Bartimaeus called out to him, using the Messianic title, " Son of David " (Luke 18:35-43). The people reprimanded him, but he called all the more until Jesus came and said, " Receive your sight; your faith has made you well." Entering Jericho, he looked up into the branches of a sycamore tree and saw a strange sight. (Ch. 19:1-10.) Zacchaeus, a wealthy tax collector, had climbed up into the tree to see Jesus. It must have been a humorous sight, but Jesus did not laugh. He said quietly, " Zacchaeus, make haste and come down; for I must stay at your house today." Zacchaeus came down, took Jesus to his home, and found God.

So the journey continued until they arrived at Bethphage and Bethany just outside of Jerusalem. There they paused while Jesus made arrangements to ride a little donkey into the city in the event that heralded the opening of his Judean ministry and the beginning of the last week of his life.

6

Judean Ministry

T HE GATHERING storm breaks with unabated fury during the last days in Judea. In contrast to the loosely knit account of the Galilean ministry and the leisurely paced record of the journey southward, the narrative now hums with excitement, Jesus and his enemies sensing that the end is near.

From now on, Jesus changes his former policy. In Galilee he had shown a definite reticence to speak of himself as the Messiah, content to proclaim the good news, explaining and demonstrating the reign of God. Now in Judea he adopts a new strategy, openly declaring his Messiahship, first through a series of symbolic acts, later directly. In a manner reminiscent of the Old Testament prophets he now deliberately acts out certain Messianic prophecies in a dramatic attempt to drive home the meaning of his vocation. His teaching during this period assumes a certain intensity, as if time is running out too soon. Hopelessly outnumbered, relentlessly pursued, Jesus makes his stand.

His friends are heroic, pathetic figures during these last days. Like small boats fighting a losing battle against the storm, they try to hold out against the tide, only to have their hopes smashed in the winds of fear and hostility. Peter, the strongest of the lot, promised to follow his Master to the death and then denied three times he had ever known him. James and John, along with Peter, followed him to the place of agony on Gethsemane, but fell asleep when he counted on them to stand watch. Most of the others scattered in panic when he was arrested. Judas betrayed him.

His enemies corner their prey and move in for the kill. Part of the time they plot with cool precision, laying traps for him and bargaining with the one who betrayed him. At other times, moving in the heat of their hatred, they strike out blindly, stirring up the people, certain of only one thing — that the man must be destroyed. Thus the stark drama moves relentlessly on to the final act of crucifixion.

The growing consciousness of filial trust and dependence that Jesus felt toward God continued as the dominant theme of his life in these last days. His ministry seemed to crumble around him, but his trust and obedience to the will of God continue to grow. The high moment arrives in the dark shadows of Gethsemane.

There is a problem of chronology involved in this Judean ministry. In the Synoptics it lasts only a week, but in John it lasts much longer. There is a good deal of evidence to support John, but in the following reconstruction we will follow the general order suggested by Mark, the earliest Gospel. This order, incidentally, is the one followed in the Christian celebration of Holy Week.

A. Entry Into Jerusalem

As they drew near to Jerusalem, Jesus sent two disciples to obtain a colt that he might use in the initiating event of the Judean ministry. (Mark 11:1-10.) Evidently arrangements had been previously worked out, for they encountered no difficulty. Bringing the colt to Jesus, they threw their garments on it, others spreading garments on the road and cutting branches from the trees. Then as Jesus rode into the city, the people shouted: " Hosanna! Blessed be he who comes in the name of the Lord! Blessed be the kingdom of our father David that is coming! Hosanna in

the highest! " Jesus rode directly into the Temple area, then re-
tired to Bethany for the night.

The crowds interpreted this as the initial event in the re-estab-
lishment of the Davidic kingdom. " Hosanna " is the equivalent
of our English, " God save the king! " Garments and branches
were thrown down as a sign of honor. In view of current glowing
Messianic hopes, the expectations of the crowd are not surprising.
When some of the Pharisees warned Jesus to silence this dangerous demonstration, he refused. " If these were silent, the very
stones would cry out," he said.

Apparently, however, the intention of Jesus was far different
from the expectation of the people. In his mind the triumphal
entry was intended as the enactment of a Messianic prophecy, but
one far from the thought of the crowd. The prophet Zechariah
had predicted the entry of the Messianic king into Jerusalem as
one who would come not as a military hero riding on a war
horse, but as a man of peace riding on a donkey. " Rejoice
greatly, O daughter of Zion! Shout aloud, O daughter of Jerusalem! Lo, your king comes to you; triumphant and victorious is
he, humble and riding on an ass, on a colt the foal of an ass."
(Zech. 9:9.) This is the prophecy which Jesus deliberately fulfilled, proclaiming in the Holy City the real character of his
Messianic vocation. By his action he declared in the very heart
and home of Israel that he was the Messiah, but a Messiah without arms or an army, a Messiah riding in humble obedience the
road marked out for the Suffering Servant of the Lord.

The crowds welcomed him as a king, but Jesus rode in as
something more than a king. Little did they realize that in less
than a week he would be dead!

B. Cleansing the Temple

Every evening Jesus took his intimate friends out to Bethany
for the night. The city was undoubtedly swarming with visitors
who had come for the Passover, and it was better to sleep away

from the noise and confusion. Moreover, it was safer to spend the night where the authorities could not find him. They were afraid to arrest him during the day, lest there be a riot among the people. They would not hesitate to seize him at night, however, if they could discover his hiding place.

On the Monday morning following the day of the triumphal entry, Jesus went back to the Temple. (Mark 11:15-19.) In the Court of the Gentiles he found a market for sacrificial animals and tables where money could be exchanged for the proper coin to pay the Temple tax. Much noise, confusion, and dishonesty attended the whole process, desecrating the holy place and causing Jesus to react swiftly in righteous anger. He drove out buyers and sellers, overturned the tables of money, and closed off the area so that it could no longer be used as a short cut through the Temple courts. Then he added ringing words from the old prophets: " Is it not written, ' My house shall be called a house of prayer for all the nations ' ? But you have made it a den of robbers." (Cf. Isa. 56:7; Jer. 7:11.)

Scholars are uncertain concerning the real intention of Jesus in this event. Some believe that he simply reacted in righteous anger when he saw the desecration of the holy place. Others feel certain that this is a second symbolic Messianic action, performed to fulfill the prophecy of Malachi who had said: " The Lord whom you seek will suddenly come to his temple. . . . But who can endure the day of his coming? . . . And he will purify the sons of Levi, and refine them like gold and silver " (Mal. 3:1-3). In this interpretation, the cleansing of the Temple becomes a symbol of the Messiah's role in purging the religion of Israel of its materialism and commercialism. This may be reading too much back into the story, but it is difficult to understand what Jesus expected to accomplish otherwise. Surely he knew the traders would be back the next day!

There have been ceaseless arguments about the anger of Jesus and the physical force that he used. The anger should not surprise us. As Augustine once remarked, we should not be surprised at the anger of a righteous man; we should look for the cause of his anger. As for the physical violence, it should be pointed out that there is no indication in the record that Jesus struck any persons. Thus the passage cannot be used, as it often is, to justify capital punishment or warfare. Any doubt about the feeling of Jesus on the matter of physical violence should be cleared away by his quick action on the night of his arrest when Peter started to wield his sword. The fight was short-lived!

It should be noted that this Temple cleansing experience sealed the fate of Jesus. It was both a challenge and a threat to the Jewish leaders and one that they could not ignore. He challenged their leadership and threatened their pockets! The Synoptics assure us that they immediately sought a way to destroy him.

C. TEACHING IN THE TEMPLE

Although the Judean ministry of Jesus lasted less than a week, some of his most significant teaching took place during his daily visits to the Temple. Tuesday and Wednesday of this last week were especially crowded with fruitful verbal interchanges with his enemies. Enraged at his acts, stung by his words, the Pharisees and Sadducees worked together to try to trap him into saying something that they could use against him. They doubtless thought it would be easy to entangle him in theological problems too subtle for his untrained mind. Under the pretense of respecting his authority as a teacher they submitted many delicate questions, expecting to impale him on the horns of a dilemma. But he always discerned their intentions and frustrated their purposes by turning the question back to them. He was able to use every situation advantageously, not only confounding his enemies, but teaching his disciples at the same time.

The first question concerned his authority. (Mark 11:27-33.) This is not surprising, since he had cleansed the Temple on the day before and had thereby openly challenged the authority of the scribes and priests. It was their duty to handle matters related to the Temple worship, certainly not the duty of an untrained teacher from Galilee! Their question, therefore, is rhetorical: "By what authority are you doing these things?" They obviously believed he had no authority. Jesus replied that he would answer if they would tell him whether the baptism of John was from heaven or of men. They dared not answer, "From heaven" because the Sanhedrin had ignored John's baptism; they dared not answer, "Of men" because the nation at large believed that John had been a true prophet of God. So they answered Jesus, "We do not know." Thus he escaped their pointed attack, at the same time implying that he regarded both his authority and John's as coming from God.

For the next question the Pharisees reinforced their own ranks with some of the Herodians and confronted him with Roman taxation, one of the burning issues of the age. (Mark 12:13-17.) The Jews rankled under the Roman tax, not only because of the money involved, but also because it was a symbol of subjection and servitude. Thus their question was shrewdly phrased: "Is it lawful to pay taxes to Caesar, or not?" If Jesus supported the tax, he would alienate his fellow Jews. If he opposed it, he would be charged with sedition and revolutionary intentions. Jesus replied by denying that this was an either/or situation: "Render to Caesar the things that are Caesar's, and to God the things that are God's." Since the tax coin belonged to Caesar anyway, there was certainly no harm in giving it back to him. But taxes or no, the important thing is to render God his due in terms of obedience and service. They were amazed at his answer, not only because he had escaped their trap, but also because he had plumbed the depths of the issue and turned their double-barbed question into a creative principle of action.

The Sadducees were the next group to enter the conflict, asking a question based on their own refusal to believe in a future life. (Mark 12:18-27.) They set up a ridiculous hypothetical situation

arising out of the levirate law (Deut. 25:5-6), which requires the
brother of a dead man who has left no child to marry the widow.
They described a woman who married seven brothers in succession and then died. "In the resurrection," they asked, "whose
wife will she be?" Expecting a materialistic reply, they were no
doubt shocked when Jesus turned the tables on them by quoting
the Torah and demonstrating both their ignorance of Scripture
and their lack of faith in the power of God. They had missed the
real point, for in the resurrection there will be no marriage as
practiced in this life.

By this time his opponents were impressed with his ability to
handle the most difficult questions. The last question, therefore,
advanced by one of the scribes, is far less antagonistic in tone.
(Mark 12:28-34.) "Which commandment," he wanted to know,
"is the first of all?" Jesus replied by combining two great commandments from the Torah: "Hear, O Israel: The Lord our
God, the Lord is one; and you shall love the Lord your God with
all your heart, and with all your soul, and with all your mind,
and with all your strength" (Deut. 6:4) and "You shall love
your neighbor as yourself" (Lev. 19:18). The ensuing friendly
conversation between Jesus and the scribe is a delightful interlude in the otherwise tense drama of the Judean ministry.

During this series of questions, the crowds expressed amazement at his answers and his enemies no longer "dared to ask
him any questions." Since they could not corner him with words,
they would have to find some other way to silence him quickly,
for affairs were rapidly getting out of hand.

D. THE BETRAYAL

Caiaphas, the high priest at this time, and Annas, his father-in-law, now enter the drama as leaders of the plot against Jesus. It
is more than doubtful, however, whether they could have ended
his career so quickly if one of his own disciples had not turned
traitor. But Judas Iscariot slipped out on Wednesday, went to

the high priest and offered to betray Jesus, thus making possible a quick, safe, and easy arrest (Mark 14:10-11). Thirty pieces of silver quickly changed hands to seal the bargain, and plans were carefully laid. There is disagreement concerning the information divulged by Judas, but two main theories are commonly proposed.

Some believe he betrayed the Messianic secret. By informing the authorities that Jesus definitely claimed to be the Messiah, he provided them with the information needed to accuse him of treason before the Roman authorities. Since Jesus had never openly declared his Messiahship, had never claimed to be " King of the Jews," there was scant evidence for a trial. When Judas provided them with this evidence they could move swiftly. The objection to this view is that the testimony provided by the witnesses at his trial fails to secure the conviction of Jesus. Why wasn't Judas called as a witness? Apparently, until Jesus convicted himself, things were going badly at the trial, leading us to conclude that only circumstantial evidence was available.

The more probable view is that Judas betrayed the place where Jesus spent each night on the Mount of Olives. In order to avoid arrest at night, Jesus remained out amid the vast crowd of religious pilgrims encamped outside the city walls. If the authorities knew where to locate him in this throng, they could arrest him quickly at night before a disturbance could break out. This theory is supported by the fact that in all the sources Judas acts as guide to those who arrest Jesus. He even kisses Jesus so that there can be no mistaken identity in the dark.

Judas Iscariot remains an enigma. What prompted him to betray Jesus? No one knows, but several motives have been suggested. (1) Some believe that he was destined to betray Jesus, but such a view raises questions about the character of God and implies that Judas had no freedom of choice. (2) It is commonly supposed that he betrayed Jesus for money. This is the motive exhibited in most Passion plays, but the sum of money involved is far too small. If Judas wanted money for betraying Jesus, he could have demanded far more than seventeen dollars! (3) Others believe that he was the only Judean among Galileans and soon became bitterly alienated from them. This view is possible, but there is little evidence to support it. (4) A popular modern view holds that Judas attempted to force Jesus into assuming a Messianic role. Judas, disappointed in the lack of decisiveness exhibited by Jesus, believed that Jesus could be forced to declare himself Messiah if pushed hard enough and threatened with execution. He had faith that Jesus could become " King of the Jews " whenever he wished and carry the nation with him. When Jesus was sentenced to die, Judas realized his scheme had failed, so he went out and killed himself. Such a view is attractive in some ways, but there is little evidence to support it. (5) The most probable theory is that the betrayal was motivated by bitterness and disappointment. Disappointed because Jesus had turned out to be a " false Messiah," Judas turned him over to the authorities.

This last view assumes that Judas, like most of his contemporaries, expected the Messiah to be a worldly military and political leader on a grand scale. Assuming that Jesus would fulfill this role, Judas had thrown in his lot with him, only to have Jesus repeatedly delay the establishment of his Kingdom. Increasingly disappointed, Judas may have felt his hopes rise momentarily when Jesus rode into Jerusalem. The moment had arrived! But once again Jesus disappointed him. Instead of initiating the rebellion, he continued to talk about suffering and death. Embittered because Jesus had misled him, angry because he had wasted time in following him, Judas turned traitor. Then when he saw the way in which Jesus conducted himself during the trial, he repented, tried unsuccessfully to break his bargain with the authorities, went out and hanged himself. The earlier words of Jesus proved prophetic: " It would have been better for that man if he had not been born."

E. THE LAST SUPPER

Two events that are of unusual significance occurred on Thursday. The first took place in the upper room where he had arranged to share a final meal with his disciples. According to the Synoptic Gospels, the meal was the Passover, the ancient Jewish observance of liberation. According to John, on the other hand, the meal occurred the day before Passover when the traditional lamb was killed. The meal was thus a kiddush, a preparatory meal held before holy days. Whichever view is correct, Jesus charged the event with profound meaning through a simple rite by which he established a new covenant between God and his people. Breaking the bread, he passed it and said, " Take; this is my body." He took a cup, and shared it saying, " This is my blood of the covenant, which is poured out for many." It is interesting to note the different emphases in the narratives of this event. Mark emphasizes the coming death of Jesus. (Mark 14:22-25.) Matthew brings in the idea of forgiveness of sins. (Matt. 26:26-29.) Luke changes the order of events. (Luke 22:15-20.) Paul, in the earliest account of the supper (I Cor. 11:23-26), adds that the covenant is a new covenant, that the rite is to be repeated, and that it should emphasize the remembrance of Jesus. These variations show that it was some time before a standard order for the Lord's Supper had been established and accepted among the early Christians.

At the beginning, the Lord's Supper was observed as a meal. Paul, for example, complained that the Corinthians ate and drank so greedily that they denied the very spirit of Christ. But by the middle of the second century, the observance had become a ceremonial rite, increasing in complexity and gathering new meaning. It would be impossible to describe this meaning in detail, but at least four major areas are obvious.

1. The remembrance of Jesus, especially of his death, is uppermost in the observance of the Lord's Supper. Human memory is

a wonderful but mysterious thing. With it we can reach back through the years and pluck things out of the past to make them vivid. But, at best, the human memory fades as the years go by, and even people we have known well and loved deeply slip from our consciousness. Jesus knew it would be like this for his disciples, and so he left them a simple rite by which their memory of him could be quickened. It reminded them in a simple dramatic way of everything he had said and done.

But especially it reminded them of his death. The early Christians were convinced that the death of Jesus had been the means by which they had become reconciled to God. Thus the remembrance of his death became an essential part of Christian worship. In the Lord's Supper the figures of speech that Jesus used, the bread and the wine symbolizing his broken body and spilled blood, and the realization that this was his last meal all combine to make the death of Christ more real to those who join in this observance.

2. Through this event, Jesus brought men into a new covenant relationship with God. The covenant had been an essential part of Jewish life. It was the binding agreement between God and Israel, resulting from God's choice of Israel in the exodus and his continuing protection through their history. By observing the law, the people of Israel upheld their end of the covenant agreement.

Jesus now introduced a new covenant into the life of man. The crucial event that gave rise to the covenant was not a new exodus but his own sacrificial death. This event leads men into a new kind of relationship with God. The conditions of the covenant are no longer expressed through the law but through a continuing experience of repentance and faith. By observing the Lord's Supper, the believer renews the new covenant relationship with God now established by Jesus. Thus observance of the Last Supper is an experience of continuing dedication.

3. The Last Supper from the beginning was a Eucharist, a

" thanksgiving." This may seem strange, since it emphasized the death of Christ, but the early Christians knew that resurrection had followed crucifixion. They began worshiping on the first day of the week, rather than the last, because Jesus had risen on that day. It was inevitable that the Lord's Supper should become a part of this weekly observance of his resurrection. Increasingly, they gave thanks for the living presence of Christ that they felt and they associated their giving of thanks with the ritual he had initiated. In this sense the Last Supper is still the Eucharist.

4. The Last Supper is a reminder of the fellowship of Christian believers. The early Christians entered into a fellowship (*koinōnia*) of life-sharing at the deepest levels. There was a love and concern for one another unlike anything they had ever known before. Paul describes it in a moving way when he says the whole fellowship rejoiced when one member felt joy and suffered when one member felt pain. Observance of the Last Supper was a continuing reminder of the strength of this unity which they had found through Christ.

No amount of theological diversity, great as that is today, can obscure the clear symbolism of fellowship present in this sacrament. There is, however, the widest possible variation in the interpretation of what actually occurs in the Last Supper. Some Christians, notably Roman Catholics, insist that the bread and wine actually become the body and blood of Jesus. Protestants cannot accept this theory of transubstantiation, but neither can they agree on an alternative interpretation. Some insist that the sacrament is strictly a memorial, a remembering of Jesus. Others accept the doctrine of the real presence (consubstantiation) in which Christ becomes " truly present " in the bread and wine, though not in bodily form. But in spite of this vast divergence of interpretation, the Lord's Supper is an expression of the oneness of all who belong to Christ. By this rite we all participate in the life of the one universal church and become a part of the body of Christ. Such an interpretation is of the greatest significance for the followers of one who came to draw all men into a common bond of love under a loving Father.

F. Gethsemane

After they had sung a hymn in the upper room, Jesus and the disciples went out to Gethsemane on the Mount of Olives to pray. (Mark 14:32-42.) Gethsemane (" oil press ") was a garden — or, more properly, an olive grove — on the lower slope of the mountain. In view of the impending crisis it is not surprising to find Jesus in a place of prayer. Now he needed even more than before to throw himself in filial trust upon the Father's love. Now was the time to seek strength for the impending crisis through an experience of direct communion with the Holy Presence. As always, also, he was seeking total submission of his will to the will of God. Taking Peter, James, and John with him to watch, he fell on the ground in an agony of prayer.

Reasons for the agony of the Gethsemane are not difficult to find. Physical suffering and death were imminent. One friend had betrayed him; other friends misunderstood him. His Messianic mission, which began with such promise in Galilee, was ending in failure. Had he misinterpreted the call that came at his baptism? Had he fulfilled God's purpose for his life? Should he run away and begin again somewhere else? All of the temptations that he had known in the wilderness may have come flooding back into his consciousness. As he wrestled with them, " his sweat became like great drops of blood falling down upon the ground."

Three times he prayed, "Father, if thou art willing, remove this cup from me." He thus expressed himself openly to the Father, seeking another way if possible. But three times also he went on to pray, "Nevertheless not my will, but thine, be done." Here was the dominant petition of his life, the wellspring of his spiritual power, the climax of his obedience to God's call. As it turned out, the opening petition was not answered, for the next day he received and drank the full cup of suffering. But the dominant petition was answered. The courage with which he faced his accusers in the next few hours was grounded on the prayer of self-surrender in Gethsemane.

In this moment we reach the climax of his conscious submission to the will of God and the fulfillment of his Messianic office. Beginning with the baptism and continuing through his whole life, including the temptation and the transfiguration, Jesus consciously related himself to God with increasing intensity until in Gethsemane his will was " one " with the will of God. Here was the final and complete surrender. The Messiah who had come to announce the reign of God became a living embodiment of that reign; the Suffering Servant of the Lord was prepared for rejection and death; the Son who had lived in absolute trust and dependence achieved the fulfillment of his filial relationship to the Father. No wonder Höffding, the Danish philosopher, called Gethsemane " the highest moment in the history of religion "!

7

Crucifixion

A FEW HOURS after the prayer in the Garden, Jesus was dead. He was arrested in haste and convicted the same night in order to complete the execution before the holy day. The story of his suffering and death was probably the first section of the Gospel material to be committed to writing on account of its importance to the faith of the early church. It is told with dignity and restraint, undoubtedly reflecting the mood of the writers and not the mood of the despairing disciples who were with him at the time.

From the beginning, the cross has occupied a place at the center of the Christian religion. An instrument of torture at first, it rapidly became a symbol of redemption. Men became convinced that through the death of Jesus their sinful lives had been redeemed or saved. The followers of Jesus could not agree on how this happened, but they were sure that it did happen. Those lost in the depths of sin and rebellion found themselves reconciled to God through the death of Christ. This is why there is always a protest when the life of the church wanders too far from the message of the cross. It is reported that an old church in Sweden has a large crucifix hanging on the back wall opposite the pulpit where only the minister sees it. When a tourist asked about it he was told that it was a gift of the king of Sweden who visited the church one Sunday, expecting to worship. Disappointed that the minister departed from his prepared manuscript in order to eulogize the king, he later sent the crucifix with instructions that it be placed at the back of the church where the minister could see it and remember that he ought to preach Christ crucified! However we look at it, the cross dominates the life story of Jesus.

A. The Trials

The moment after the prayer in the Garden when Jesus went to rouse his sleeping disciples, Judas appeared at the head of a mob sent by the Jewish authorities. (Mark 14:43-52.) Jesus protested his secret arrest at night when he might have been taken any day in the Temple, and one of his followers resisted by wounding a member of the arresting mob with his sword. " All who take the sword will perish by the sword," said Jesus, ending the fight before it began. He allowed himself to be taken without a struggle, and the moment the leader was captured the followers scattered in panic.

After a preliminary examination before Annas, Jesus was taken before the Sanhedrin, the highest court of justice and supreme council in Jerusalem. (Mark 14:53-72.) Many witnesses were heard, but their testimony broke down under cross-examination. Under Jewish law, a capital conviction was impossible unless the testimony of two witnesses was in agreement. Things were going from bad to worse for the prosecution until the high priest suddenly asked Jesus directly, " Are you the Christ, the Son of the Blessed? " Up to this point Jesus had remained silent, but he now answered, " I am." The high priest tore his garment in a dramatic gesture of horror, and from this moment Jesus was treated as a condemned man. " Some began to spit on him, and to cover his face, and to strike him, saying to him, ' Prophesy! ' And the guards received him with blows."

The main charge in this trial had been blasphemy, the taking upon himself prerogatives belonging to God. His accusers had claimed that he had forgiven sins, broken the Sabbath law and the law of fasting, threatened the Temple, and claimed future glory for himself as the Messiah. Ordinarily, a condemned blasphemer was stoned, but under Roman rule the Jews had no right to pronounce the death sentence. At dawn, therefore, they took him before Pontius Pilate. (Mark 15:2-15.)

The Roman authorities had no interest in the charge of blasphemy, but they could not ignore a prisoner with political aspirations. For this reason, Jesus was charged with treason, as we see in Pilate's first question: " Are you the King of the Jews? " Even though he did not obtain a satisfactory answer, Pilate would not condemn Jesus. He was apparently favorably impressed by his prisoner, for he exhibited obvious reluctance in pronouncing the death sentence.

Only Luke tells of the trial before Herod. (Luke 23:6-16.) When Pilate heard that Jesus was a Galilean, he sent him before Herod Antipas who was in Jerusalem for the Passover. Herod's enmity was changed to friendship by this gesture, though Pilate was probably simply trying to find a way out of a tight situation. Herod, filled with curiosity, soon became infuriated when Jesus refused to answer his questions. After clothing the prisoner in royal robes to ridicule his alleged kingship, he returned him to Pilate.

Still, Pilate tried to avoid the death sentence by giving the crowd the opportunity to free Jesus or Barabbas, resorting to an annual custom observed at the time of Passover. When they cried for Barabbas, Pilate asked what they would have done with Jesus. " And they cried out again, ' Crucify him.' And Pilate said to them, ' Why, what evil has he done? ' But they shouted all the more, ' Crucify him.' " According to Matthew, Pilate then took a basin of water and tried to wash his hands of the whole business, after which he released Barabbas and delivered Jesus to be crucified.

Did Jesus have a fair trial? Obviously not, for the whole affair was rushed through with great haste, in an atmosphere of mob rule rather than calm deliberation. Through the entire proceeding we feel the rising temper of the mob and the confused perplexity of Pilate. Finally, he surrendered to the will of the crowd, the life of one peasant a small price to pay for preservation of the peace.

During Jesus' trial before the Sanhedrin, Peter had an unfortunate experience. Apparently the only disciple courageous enough to follow Jesus to the high priest's house, he was warming himself at a fire when one of the maids recognized him. Peter denied that he was a follower of Jesus, but she identified him again by the gate. Again he denied it. A bystander also challenged him and Peter denied it with a curse. But when he heard a cock crowing he remembered that Jesus had warned him about his weakness, and he wept. This is a very human story, so like the Peter who appears throughout the Gospels, and it was probably included in the Passion story from the beginning to emphasize the loneliness of Jesus in his hour of suffering. Judas had betrayed him, the others fled, and now Peter, the " rock," denied him!

B. Crucifixion

The role of Suffering Servant now falls upon Jesus without mercy or relief. (Mark 15:21-41.) He was scourged and beaten time and again. Ordinarily, for this purpose, leather whips with sharp pieces of metal tied at the ends were used in order to tear the prisoner's flesh. They spat on him, mocked him, pressed a crown of thorns upon his head, and forced him to carry the heavy cross along the Via Dolorosa, the " way of sorrow," which led to Golgotha. As they passed along the road, Simon of Cyrene, a Jew from North Africa who was coming into the city, was compelled to carry the cross. The loss of blood and the exhaustion of the sleepless night may partially explain the failure of Jesus' physical strength.

The place of execution, Golgotha, means " skull " place, and may have been named because of its shape or because of the number of deaths that had taken place there. It was the common custom to execute prisoners in public places outside the city as a warning to others. Two thieves were executed with Jesus.

When they arrived at Golgotha, Jesus was stripped of his clothing and nailed, hands and feet, to the cross. He was offered wine as an opiate, but refused it. His garments went by lot to the soldiers who had brought dice to pass the time while waiting for the death of the prisoners. An inscription was placed over the cross as a warning to others. Though the wording differs in the Gospel reports, the general charge is clear: " The King of the Jews." Soldiers, bystanders, and even one of the dying thieves join in reviling Jesus.

In the four Gospels seven last words of Jesus are recorded. Mark and Matthew include only the cry, " My God, my God, why hast thou forsaken me? " This has given commentators a good deal of difficulty, since it sounds like utter despair. Many believe, however, that Jesus is identifying himself with the sufferer in Ps. 22. This is a direct quote from the opening lines of that psalm which closes with an expression of faith. The psalmist is saying that, though God seems to forsake the sufferer, he never does. This may well have been the mood of Jesus in this hour.

Luke adds three words. " Father, forgive them; for they know not what they do," does not appear in some important manuscripts, but it is certainly in keeping with the spirit of Jesus' life and teaching. " Truly, I say to you, today you will be with me in Paradise," was spoken to the repentant criminal who recognized that God should be feared and his own sins punished. " Father, into thy hands I commit my spirit! " is the final cry of Jesus, a fitting end for the life of one who had lived fully under the reign of God.

The three other words are found only in John's Gospel. Some of the women and John Zebedee were standing near the cross, so Jesus asked John to provide a home for his mother after his death: " Woman, behold your son! . . . Behold your mother! " The terrible pangs of thirst tormented Jesus on the cross and he

cried, "I thirst." It is worth noting that the Gospel most concerned about the divinity of Jesus records this most human cry
from the cross. Finally, the last word according to John is a cry,
not of despair, but of triumphant accomplishment: "It is finished." He had completed the work that God had given him
to do.

The enemies who thus crucified him would not have believed
anyone who suggested that the cruel device for torture on which
he died would become for countless persons the supreme symbol
of God's power and love. This, however, is exactly what happened. In view of this strange transformation, we should examine
briefly the doctrine of the atonement through which Christians
have tried to explain this significance of the cross.

The followers of Jesus believe that man has become estranged
from God because of sin, but that God has done something
about this situation through the life, teaching, and death of Jesus.
The cross, especially, is God's way of seeking reconciliation (at-
one-ment) with man, hence the doctrine of the atonement. The
way in which reconciliation is accomplished through the death
of Jesus has been a matter of dispute, but three main theories have
been proposed.

For the first ten centuries, most Christians held the ransom
theory of the atonement, according to which sinful men were
held in bondage by the devil. The only way God could release
men was by paying a ransom to the devil, and the only ransom
price high enough was the life of God's own Son. Thus God let
Jesus die as a ransom paid to the devil to secure the release of
sinful men. Even though attempts were made to allegorize this
rather crude belief, it implies that God is forced to bargain with
the devil and then "deceive the great deceiver" by taking the
ransom back on Easter Day. Since the eleventh century, therefore, most Christians have held either a substitutionary or a moral
theory of the atonement.

According to the substitutionary view, Christ died as a substitute for men who deserve punishment because of their sin. Sin is a dishonoring of God, and man, hopelessly caught in a life of sin, has no way of requiting God's honor. Hence, it was necessary for the Son of God to die as a substitute. This is a widely held view, but it leaves at least two serious questions unanswered. What kind of God would demand such requited honor or would demand the death of his own Son in order to be "satisfied"? How can anyone assume the guilt of another person? Suffering, it is true, can be borne by others, but not guilt.

The moral theory of the atonement insists that the obstacle to man's reconciliation with God is sinfulness. God is eager to forgive and receive all of his children in love, but their continuing disobedience prevents this fellowship with him. If only man's rebellious will could be brought into true repentance, then God would respond in forgiving love, and reconciliation would be accomplished. This is exactly what takes place through the crucifixion.

In the first place the cross brings men to repentance because it involves them in sin at its worst. They see what pride, indifference, insensitivity, selfishness, and cruelty can do. Swept up into this event, a man sees his sin for what it is until he can no longer bear it. This is illustrated by the attitude of the inhabitants of a medieval European city visited by the plague. Since they had known the plague before, they refused to talk about the new epidemic. A law was passed, punishing anyone who mentioned it. As the plague grew worse they began to talk about it in disguised tones, finally even admitting it was a "sort of plague." Only when people were dropping like flies did they finally admit it was the plague and start to do something about it. Because of what he experiences through the cross, the Christian stops ignoring and disguising his sinfulness. He sees and feels and knows it for what it is and turns in repentance to God.

In the second place, however, the cross is a demonstration of love at its best, a demonstration of what the love of God can mean. Here in the crucifixion man becomes involved in that which God does to bring men into a relationship of loving fellowship with Him. It is the culminating revelation of the love of God that illuminated and empowered the entire life of Jesus. Those witnessing and experiencing this love can appreciate the question of the small boy about to undergo an operation who looked up at his father just before receiving the anesthetic and asked, " You'll go all the way with me, won't you, Daddy? " The Christian feels that in the crucifixion God has gone all the way with sinful man in offering his forgiving love. This love of God calls forth from man a trustful acceptance of the forgiveness of God that completes the act of reconciliation. Through repentance, therefore, and the confident acceptance of the forgiving love of God, man achieves reconciliation. This experience of atonement is made possible through the cross of Christ.

Like the other theories of atonement, this view has certain weaknesses. It is especially weak when watered down to a point where the cross simply becomes a courageous example set by a courageous man. On the contrary, the moral theory at its best emphasizes the uniqueness of this reconciling act of God and the necessity of man's entering into this event to such a degree that he is transformed. He not only *feels* different, he *is* different, a " new creature " as the apostle Paul would have it, a " new being " as Paul Tillich has called it.

Every theory of the atonement is based upon a full comprehension of the suffering and degradation endured by Jesus on the cross. We who make crosses of gold and precious stones find it almost impossible to realize that the cross was one of the most abominable forms of torture ever devised. The condemned person, lacerated by the preliminary beatings and exposed to the curses of the crowd, could not even move to brush away the insects that swarmed over his torn flesh. Dying slowly of exposure and gradual strangulation, he knew the combined anguish of physical torture and mental degradation. The length of time involved, combined with the unbearable physical pain and mental anguish, recommended this form of execution to those who delighted in torture.

Thus died God's Messiah about the ninth hour in a scene of unrelieved tragedy. He had received the dreaded cup of suffering filled to overflowing.

C. Burial

Mercifully, Jesus died sooner than expected at crucifixion. (Mark 15:42-47.) According to John, a spear was thrust in his side to make certain death had come. Burial had to be completed quickly, for the Sabbath would begin at sunset. All four of the Gospels agree that a certain Joseph of Arimathea asked Pilate for the body and then took it to his own new tomb, which had been hewn out of a rock. Joseph was a follower of Jesus and a member of the Sanhedrin. The body was wrapped in a linen shroud temporarily until the women could return after the Sabbath and prepare it with spices and ointments for permanent burial.

When the body had been laid within the tomb, Joseph placed a stone in front of the entrance, presumably a large circular stone that rolled in a groove in front of the doorway. Some of the women who had followed him from Galilee, including Mary Magdalene, saw where they had put him.

The women then went to make their preparations. The disciples felt the full weight of despair resulting from their crumbled hopes and their shattered dreams. The Romans went about their official business of keeping the peace. The Pharisees slept untroubled at last. All were certain beyond any doubt that the end had come.

8

Resurrection

THE MOOD of the disciples on the eve of the resurrection was one of shocked disbelief and bitter disappointment. At first they could not bring themselves to believe that it had ended this way. Then, slowly, they began to feel sorry for themselves. God had let them down.

This latter feeling would be hard to describe to those who have never felt thus abandoned, but it must have been something like the experience of one well-known contemporary figure on the evening of President Eisenhower's first inauguration. Old William C. Handy, the father of the blues, had been invited to join the group of entertainers who would play for President and Mrs. Eisenhower on their great night. He was old now, blind, and he hadn't played his trumpet for a long while. But he would play for the President! His life, which had begun in poverty and obscurity, would now reach its highest moment at the inaugural ball in Washington.

In preparation for the great night he bought a new suit, polished his trumpet, and practiced. He would be ready. But when the night came there was a great deal of confusion. The entertainment schedule fell behind as President and Mrs. Eisenhower traveled back and forth between the ballrooms of two hotels. Bill Handy waited quietly, unable to see, but feeling the excitement all around him. At last he was introduced. When he had played two choruses of his most famous song, "The St. Louis Blues," he sat down exhausted, and there was such a look of radiant happiness on his face that no one had the heart to tell him until later that President Eisenhower had left the ballroom a half hour before. The great moment of his life, playing his best music for the President, but the President wasn't even there to hear him!

The disciples must have been even more tragically disappointed, for they felt abandoned by God. They had given up everything — family, homes, and work — to follow Jesus who had spoken so confidently of God's loving concern for them. He had told them that the reign of God was at hand, and he had urged them to become reconciled to God and live a new life of love while they awaited his coming. They had followed him faithfully and hopefully, even to Jerusalem, when they knew how dangerous that would be. And now the end had come, tragically, unexpectedly, irrevocably. God had abandoned them.

Then an utterly unbelievable thing happened. Early in the morning on the first day of the week they discovered the empty tomb, and before the day was over they knew that Jesus was alive! They refused to trust their own senses at first. Peter and John ran to the tomb to see for themselves. Thomas would not believe until he had touched Jesus. But before long they all knew that it was incredibly true. Their Lord had risen from the dead!

The resurrection of Jesus is undoubtedly the best-known event in the life of Jesus and the least understood. It is assumed that every Christian accepts the fact of the resurrection, whereas, as a matter of fact, many Christians accept it only with reservations and sometimes only in sheer blind faith. It is often treated as if it were a doctrinal belief about Jesus, but nothing could be farther from the New Testament attitude toward the event, as we shall see. Few things are needed more in Christendom than clarification of this unique event which in a very real way authenticates the entire life and ministry of Jesus.

A. Documentary Evidence

There are at least six primary documentary sources for the resurrection event. It should be emphasized here at the beginning that every source treats it as an event and not as a belief or doctrine. This was something given in experience, not simply something believed. It happened *to the disciples,* unexpectedly breaking in upon their disappointment and despair. We do not begin to understand the resurrection until we see it in this light. Certainly, all our documents speak of it as just such an experienced event.

The earliest documentary evidence is furnished by Paul. (I Cor. 15:3 f.) Writing about A.D. 55, Paul reminds the Corinthians of the tradition that he had received, presumably after his own conversion. This record, coming from the first decade after the crucifixion, is the earliest narrative of the event. Sometimes called " the oldest Christian document we possess," it lists six appearances of the risen Lord.

For I delivered to you as of first importance what I also received, that Christ died for our sins in accordance with the scriptures, that he was buried, that he was raised on the third day in accordance with scriptures, and that he appeared to Cephas, then to the twelve. Then he appeared to more than five hundred brethren at one time, most of whom are still alive, though some have fallen asleep. Then he appeared to James, then to all the apostles. Last of all, as to one untimely born, he appeared also to me.

Notice that Paul places the appearance to himself on the same level with all the others.

Mark's Gospel (ch. 16:1-8) describes how the women found the empty tomb, how a young man told them of the risen Jesus, and how they fled in fear. The majority of scholars agree that the original ending of this Gospel has been lost. Undoubtedly in its unmutilated form it contained an appearance of the risen Lord, for it predicted such an appearance five times in the earlier portion of the Gospel.

Matthew's Gospel (ch. 28:1-20) describes the finding of the empty tomb and then records two appearances of Jesus, to the women who visited the tomb and to the eleven apostles on the mountain in Galilee.

Luke (ch. 24:1-53) relates how the women, after finding the tomb empty, brought the news to the incredulous eleven. He then records three appearances, to the two disciples on the road to Emmaus, to Peter, and to the group of disciples in Jerusalem.

John (chs. 20:1 to 21:25) relates how Mary Magdalene found the tomb empty and how Peter and John visited the tomb to confirm her report. He then records four appearances, to Mary Magdalene in the garden, to ten disciples behind closed doors on the same day, to ten disciples and Thomas a week later, to seven disciples on the shore of the lake in Galilee.

Any compilation of sources for the resurrection should also include the early sermons in the book of The Acts. Though written down by Luke late in the first century, these faithfully capture the spirit of the earliest Christian message (kerygma). And all agree in emphasizing the experienced fact of the resurrection. Peter, for example, strictly charged by the Jerusalem authorities to preach no more, could not be silent and answered them in no uncertain terms: " The God of our fathers raised Jesus whom you killed by hanging him on a tree. God exalted him at his right hand as Leader and Savior, to give repentance to Israel and forgiveness of sins. And we are witnesses to these things, and so is the Holy Spirit whom God has given to those who obey him " (Acts 5:30-32).

A careful reading of this material reveals what may at first seem to be a troubling disagreement on details. It is impossible, for example, to weave a consistent account of who went to the tomb early in the morning. Nor can we determine with accuracy whom they met or what was said when they first discovered that the tomb was empty. Each of the documents gives a different account of where Jesus appeared. Such discrepancies have caused some commentators to question the essential validity of the documentary reports.

Actually, however, the more we think about the nature of this event, the less surprising we find such divergent reports. The disciples were already in a state of shock when this thing broke upon them. Then they found themselves raised to a level of joy and excitement higher than any they had known before. No wonder they described the details of their experience in different ways! In reality the discrepancies help authenticate the documents, for it is obvious that no harmonizing process has been allowed to work here.

The important thing, however, is the absolute agreement of all sources on the fact of the resurrection as an experienced event. There is apparently some doubt about the empty tomb, it is true. Paul does not seem to know about it, and Mark's Gospel belittles its importance. But all agree on the one basic fact: Jesus, whom they had known and whom they had seen dead and buried, was alive again. They agree on this basic fact because it was an experienced fact. It was something that happened to them, a given reality that transformed the blackness of their despair into radiant joy.

Someone once asked William James if he believed in infant baptism. Looking surprised, he replied: "Believe in it. Why, man, I've seen it!" The early disciples would look just as surprised if asked, "Do you believe in the resurrection?" It was not a matter of believing in it, for they had seen it, known it, experienced it. On this fundamental fact, all our documentary sources agree.

B. CIRCUMSTANTIAL EVIDENCE

There is a large body of evidence based on the circumstances that surrounded the resurrection event. Taken alone, such evidence does not prove that the resurrection actually occurred, but it does add great weight to the other evidence available.

The existence of the Christian church attests the authenticity of the resurrection. The church was founded on the belief that Jesus was the Messiah, but a crucified Messiah was no Messiah at all. The fellowship of Christians that developed into an organized church was organized around a living Messiah, a living Savior. They did not gather to hold memorial services for a dead founder, but communion services with a living Lord. If the crucifixion had ended the life of Jesus, it is impossible to account for the birth, growth, and continuing existence of the Christian church.

The existence of the New Testament cannot be accounted for apart from the fact of the resurrection. It is hard to see how anyone would have bothered to write anything about a dead Messiah. The author of every single one of the twenty-seven New Testament documents is positively convinced that Jesus rose from the dead and continues to live in the fellowship of believers. The fact that the New Testament came into being at all and the fact that it became " Scripture " attest the validity of the resurrection event.

The observance among Christians of Sunday as the weekly day of worship is further circumstantial evidence that Jesus rose from the dead. Most of the early Christians had been Jews for whom the sacred day was the Sabbath or seventh day of the week. In spite of the sacred tradition surrounding this day, however, the followers of Jesus changed their sacred day from the seventh to the first day of the week because they were certain that Jesus had risen on that day. There is no possible way to account for this fundamental change apart from their remembrance of having first experienced the presence of the risen Lord on that day.

Finally, the joyous celebration of the Eucharist is inexplicable apart from the resurrection. As we have seen, this sacrament commemorates the death of Jesus, yet it is a rite in which there is no mourning for the dead. On the contrary, the dominant note of the Eucharist is joyful gratitude. The word "Eucharist" means "thanksgiving." If the death of Jesus had not been followed by his resurrection, it would be difficult to account for the continued observance of the Eucharist, and it would be impossible to account for its joyous character.

Thus the church's Scripture, its day of worship, its chief act of worship, as well as its very existence, constitute an impressive array of evidence to support the Christian conviction that Jesus rose from the dead.

C. Experiential Evidence

In every age, including our own, the strongest evidence for the resurrection may be found in the realm of personal experience. This is possible because the Jesus who lived, died, and lived again is not simply a dead figure remembered from the past. He is a living figure who is known still. The resurrection was real to the earliest disciples because it was an experienced event. It was real to Paul, though he probably never saw Jesus in the flesh, as an experienced event. In exactly the same way it becomes real to us.

This is not to say that we all have blinding visions of the risen Lord. But we do experience the Holy Spirit who manifests himself within the community of faith as the living Christ. Countless Christians across the years have known him in this way. We do not ultimately accept the fact of the resurrection because of first-century experiences reported in the New Testament. We accept it because it is a fact of our own experience; it is a something that happens to us. Our own conviction of the resurrection ultimately rests on this continuing certainty of his continuing presence in the community of faith.

Those who have had no such experience find it hard, if not impossible, to believe this kind of argument from personal experience. It cannot be scientifically demonstrated; it cannot be adequately described. But it is the strongest evidence of all for the one who has experienced it. There is a self-authenticating quality about experiential evidence of this type. Suddenly we *know* what the early disciples were trying to say about the risen Jesus, for we have known him too.

The nature of this evidence gives rise to a strange sort of paradox, however. In spite of all the documentary and circumstantial evidence supporting the resurrection, no one has a right to expect us to accept it unconditionally until we have known Christ in our own experience. We may in all honesty reserve final judgment on this matter until the resurrection becomes a fact given to us. On the other hand, no one has a right to deny the resurrection until he has placed himself within the environment where Christ can be thus known, namely, within the community of faith. What right do we have to deny the fact of the resurrection if we have ignored the source of the most convincing evidence? This paradox applies especially to so many modern young people who find it difficult, if not impossible, to believe in the resurrection on the basis of the New Testament. The church cannot expect these young persons to accept the resurrection fully until they have known Christ as a living presence themselves. On the other hand, these same young persons cannot categorically deny the fact of the resurrection if they have not placed themselves in the community of faith where he can be known.

The documentary evidence for the resurrection is unusually convincing for an event of this kind. The circumstantial evidence adds great weight to the certainty of the documents. But the most convincing evidence of all is the present experience of those who discover that Jesus is not a dead figure from the past who is remembered still. He is a living Lord who is *known* still.

D. Unanswered Questions

The fact of the resurrection is the most vital issue involved in any discussion of this unique event. As we have seen, there is an abundance of convincing evidence supporting the fact. Unfortunately, however, there are important questions that remain unanswered even after the most careful reading of the narrative reports. Two such questions especially plague those seeking a coherent picture of this event. What was the nature of the resurrection body? What happened to the physical body?

In answer to the first question, many persons are convinced that the resurrection body was the resuscitated physical body. According to this view, we can account for the fact that Jesus ate with the disciples, invited them to touch him, and disappeared from the tomb. On the other hand, if Jesus appeared in physical form, how do we account for his mysterious appearance in closed rooms, for the fact that the disciples did not recognize him at first (cf. the two disciples who walked seven miles to Emmaus with him without recognizing him!), and for the undisturbed graveclothes? Also, what happened to this physical body? According to Luke, he ascended bodily to heaven, a view acceptable to the ancients with their several-storied universe but unacceptable to most moderns.

At the other extreme are those who believe that the disciples simply had visions of Christ. According to this view, the tremendous impact of his personality caused the disciples to " remember him " with special vividness after he had left them. Such a personality could not be conquered by death. Many supporters of this view insist that the visions were " God-given," thus having an objective basis, but were, nonetheless, visions. One difficulty with this theory, however, is that it does not accord with the documentary evidence. These reported experiences were real experiences of some kind. Five hundred people (as reported by Paul) do not have a common vision all at the same time. The chief difficulty, however, is that the psychological conditions necessary for a visionary experience were not present. Before such visions occur, men are usually " on tiptoe with expectation." The resurrection came as a complete surprise. The disciples would not even believe it at first, treating it as an " idle tale." This is hardly the material of which visions are made!

Because of the difficulties in these two views, many persons believe that the resurrection body of Jesus was a " spiritual body." One of the strongest arguments against immortality is that the mind and body are so interrelated that when the body dies the mind must die also. Paul gives the best answer to this argument (I Cor., ch. 15) when he says that the God who gave all forms of life here on earth an appropriate body can obviously be trusted to give an appropriate spiritual body in the next life. Very little can be said about the exact nature of this spiritual body, but many persons believe that it is the form of the resurrection body of Jesus. In some ways it was the same body; in some ways it was not. This view accounts for both types of evidence. This may well be what John had in mind when he reported that the graveclothes were undisturbed, and what Paul had in mind when he described his own experience of the risen Lord in the same breath as that in which he spoke of the experiences of the early disciples, though the physical body had disappeared long before Paul wrote. This view accords well with the existing evidence, but obviously will not appeal to those dissatisfied with the nebulous concept of a " spiritual body."

What happened to the physical body? Attempts to account for its disappearance have given rise to numerous theories. (1) The physical body ascended to heaven. (The modern view of the universe makes this difficult to accept.) (2) The physical body was transmuted into a spiritual body. (Though note that Paul never says a transmuted physical body is necessary to account for the presence of a spiritual body.) (3) The disciples stole it. (Even a Jewish scholar such as Rabbi Klausner finds this impossible to believe.) (4) The Jews or Romans disposed of it. (Scarcely possible, since they would have produced it later to refute the resurrection claims.) (5) The women went to the wrong tomb. (Ever since the Garden of Eden we have been trying to lay the blame on a woman!) (6) The body was cast into a common burial ground. (Contrary to all available evidence.) (7) We don't know.

(Perhaps the most reasonable attitude in view of our complete lack of information.)

The nature of the resurrection body and the disposition of the physical body thus remain unanswered questions. It should be emphasized, however, that the limitations of our knowledge in these areas in no way detract from our certainty of the resurrection event itself. It is unfortunate that some persons become so embroiled in the uncertainties of these unanswered questions that they miss the certainty of the one most important answered question — the Messiah's conquest of death.

E. Significance of the Resurrection

From the beginning, the resurrection has been a favorite subject in poetry, painting, and preaching as well as in music, drama, and meditation. We have already seen how it accounts for the existence of the Christian church and the New Testament, for the observance of Sunday worship and the Eucharist. It also accounts largely for the nature of the Christian hope in the future life. Ultimately, what we believe about existence after death depends upon what we know about the character of God. The resurrection of Jesus is therefore not the only ground for the Christian's hope in the future, as many Easter sermons and even Paul might lead us to believe. "If Christ has not been raised," said Paul, "your faith is futile and you are still in your sins. Then those also who have died in Christ have perished. If in this life we who are in Christ have only hope, we are of all men most to be pitied." (I Cor. 15:17-19.) What Paul is actually affirming in a statement like this is not that his faith in a future life is based solely on a belief in Christ's resurrection, but simply that his faith is grounded in the certainty of his own experience of the risen Lord. Paul's hope for the future life and ours is grounded in the power and love of God. The resurrection is significant because of the concrete and historical revelation of that power and love breaking into the life of men.

The greatest significance of the resurrection, however, is often overlooked by those attempting to interpret it in fine arts and even in religion. This event is God's authentication of Jesus. By means of the resurrection, God reversed the decision of the cross and placed his seal of approval on that which Jesus had come to say and to do. The reign of God as preached by Jesus, the nature of reconciliation and the new life, the ethic of love, all these take on added meaning because of the resurrection. After this event men realized that in the words of Jesus on these matters we have God's answer to man's dilemma. Similarly, the resurrection authenticates the actions of Jesus, the decisions he made, the truth he revealed through his life, his suffering and his death. Through this event we understand what John meant when he said, " No one has ever seen God; the only Son, who is in the bosom of the Father, he has made him known " (John 1:18).

The growing filial trust that Jesus knew throughout his life was thus fulfilled when the Father made him victor over death. He knew himself to be the Son of God in a way unknown to the other sons and daughters of God. Filled with this sense of God-consciousness, growing in obedience to God's will, he had heard the voice of God speaking at his baptism, " Thou art my beloved Son; with thee I am well pleased." Peter heard the same Voice speaking on the Mount of Transfiguration: " This is my beloved Son; listen to him." Through the resurrection God reveals the same truth to all men: " This is my beloved Son; listen to him! "

During a lull in the fighting on Heartbreak Ridge in the Korean War, several soldiers were talking with a chaplain. They fell to discussing the meaning of their dilemma and the reason for the horror of another war. One of the boys said heatedly: " I'll tell you the reason, Chaplain. Your God has let us down! " The early disciples felt this way, and many men have felt this way since. But the resurrection event continues to break into our human experience with the certainty that God has not let us down. He revealed the nature of his love through Jesus Christ and then authenticated that revelation through an event unique in the history of man. The life and teaching of Jesus, authenticated through the resurrection, is God's answer to man's dilemma, God's design for man's disorder and despair.

THE TEACHING OF JESUS

9

Jesus as Teacher

THE SAYINGS of Jesus preserved in the Gospels embody such profound truths in such a striking form that Jesus has often been called history's greatest teacher. Without doubt he was, but persons who hold this view should beware of giving the impression that this is all he was.

We have already emphasized the prominent role that he assigned to teaching in his ministry. As Messiah, his main function was to proclaim the reign of God, and this inevitably involved a great deal of teaching. But he was not merely a teacher. Those who see in him nothing more than a great teacher miss the main point of the Gospels. He was first and foremost not teacher but Messiah, the "anointed one," the one sent by God to proclaim the good news of the reign of God. Thus his teachings are of crucial significance, but so are other phases of his Messianic ministry. Healing, companionship with the disciples, preaching, suffering, dying, rising again — all these are essential elements in the complete portrait of Jesus as Messiah. In order to keep a sense of perspective while reading his words, it is well to remember that, though he was history's greatest teacher, he was not merely a teacher.

It is also necessary to emphasize the fact that the life and teaching of Jesus can never be separated. For practical reasons it is possible to break the material down into manageable proportions, but we must point out the danger of trying to isolate the words or teaching of Jesus. More than any teacher in history, he demonstrated through his life the meaning of his teaching. To put it another way, the teaching literally grew out of his life and the life fulfilled the teaching.

In contrast, most other great teachers are not usually remembered for the example set by their lives. Socrates, one of history's greatest teachers, is often compared with Jesus. But apart from his noble death what do we remember about him? It is primarily his teaching that lives on, enshrined by Plato in the *Dialogues*. Socrates, the man, is a dim figure out of the distant past.

Not so with Jesus. It is true that his teaching is often studied entirely apart from his life, especially by those who look upon him simply as a great teacher and nothing more. But his words were so intimately related to his deeds that no one can possibly understand one without the other. Consider his words on forgiveness and nonretaliation. He told his followers not to resist one who is evil, but to turn the other cheek, to go the second mile, to love enemies and pray for them. Forgive not one time, nor even seven times (to Peter's dismay!), but seventy times seven times! What is more difficult than this? Yet on the cross Jesus looked down at those who were murdering him and prayed, "Father, forgive them; for they know not what they do." Once again, as in so many cases, his own life furnishes the supreme illustration of his own matchless teaching.

In the following chapters, therefore, we will never lose sight of his life while seeking the meaning of his message. But our main emphasis will be clear. What did he say that caused such joy, consternation, and excitement among his hearers? What was the message he preached that the authorities found so intolerable? How was he able to get his ideas across so effectively? These are the questions we ask as we turn to Jesus, the teacher, first seeking to characterize his teaching in a general way.

A. The Character of His Teaching

The teaching of Jesus was *informal*, wholly instinctive and spontaneous in style and form. There was no artificial tone in his message, no evidence of straining to create effect. He did not try to dazzle or confound his hearers through the brilliance of his rhetorical eloquence. He had the ability to find the most direct and effective expression for the most profound ideas. The plan of his teaching was also informal and never preconceived. The subjects with which he dealt were suggested to him as he went along the way, by the circumstances of daily life, by the questions of his followers, by the objections of his enemies. Each one of his sayings was the overflow of a personality throbbing with life. The setting or background of the teaching was informal and constantly changing. Sometimes he taught in the synagogue, but more often out by the lake, on the side of a hill, seated at the dinner table, or walking along the road.

His teaching was *artistic*. He presented every idea in a rich setting that made it unforgettable. Instead of beginning with abstract definitions as so many teachers do, he used a wealth of imagery to give a concrete character to his ideas. He painted word pictures, knowing that his hearers would " see " the picture long after they had forgotten his words. He could mix consolation and scorn, joy and sorrow, seriousness and humor. Everywhere he was the artist with words, manifesting his creative originality.

His teaching was *clear*. This was because it was direct, simple, and to the point. Every word hit the target, clarifying rather than obscuring the central idea. He went straight to the heart of every issue, ignoring all nonessentials. Modern poets, playwrights, preachers, and professors who revel in verbosity and obscurity might well take a leaf from his book. Both the intelligentsia and the simple-minded heard him gladly because he spoke with clarity in order to be understood.

His teaching was *authoritative*. The professional teachers of his time confined their teaching largely to comments on the text of Scripture and quotations from the tradition of the past. Jesus taught in marked contrast to these scribes, speaking directly in the name of God and with the authority coming from his sense of vocation. The Gospels tell us how the crowds marveled at the strength of his authority, hungry for teaching that had about it an atmosphere of reality and authenticity. The sense of filial trust that Jesus felt toward God made it possible for him to speak with the authority of one who came from God.

His teaching was *compelling*. He always dealt with the vital issues of life, the issues of life and death faced by all his hearers. What is the purpose of life? How can we live with one another? How can we find joy? Where are we going after we die? Why do we suffer? Jesus dealt with such problems and he did so in a way that demanded decision and action. He was constantly exhorting people to " come," " go," " follow," " heal," " love," " repent," " pray. . . ." His teaching brought men face to face with the vital issues of life, revealed God's truth, and then compelled them to decide for it or against it, once and for all.

Finally, his teaching was *existential*. No two existentialists can agree on just what this popular modern philosophy stands for, but one thing is clear. All the existentialists, from atheists to Christians, are protesting against the modern tendency of individuals to become mere " spectators " in the game of life. So many persons are content to sit on the side lines, speculating and commenting wisely on the meaning of life. But the existentialists call us down out of the stands into the game, insisting that we are all participants, not spectators. As a participant, they insist, the only thing ultimately real to me about life is the thing that is real to me *now* in this moment of my existence. Not the lost opportunities of yesterday nor the possible disasters of tomorrow, but this day alone has reality. In this sense the teaching of Jesus is existential, for he constantly called his hearers to the urgent consideration of the present moment. Where do you stand *now* in your relationship to God and to others? Are you living your life *now* in all its fullness and wonder and joy? In this way at least, Jesus was an existentialist centuries before the existentialists.

B. Methods of Teaching

The teaching of Jesus has come down to us through the Gospels in several different forms. There are, for example, short sayings, shocking paradoxes, longer discourses, and unforgettable parables. Like a skillful surgeon, Jesus knew which instrument to use to do the work at hand most effectively.

The parable is undoubtedly the best-known technique that he used. Although he did not create the parable, he perfected it as a method of teaching. A parable may be defined as a simple story from everyday life used to illustrate a religious truth. The subjects of the stories that Jesus used in his parables reveal his familiarity with the everyday life of the people around him. He spoke of lilies and tares, of nesting birds and mother hens, of children playing and men working, of treasures and pearls, of runaway sons and foolish bridesmaids, of full barns and hungry beggars, of shepherds and widows and thieves. His simple stories about such subjects suddenly made profound religious truths come alive. By this means he helped common, uneducated people understand the nature of God, the purpose of God, the meaning of life, and the power of love.

The parables were so effective because they were concrete and easy to remember. Abstract thinking has a place in man's life, but Jesus knew that abstract thinking often loses touch with reality. He therefore taught concretely, putting his thought into a form that fed the whole life of man, not just his mind. By using stories, he also made it difficult for men to forget what he said. Long after some men had forgotten his exact words, they could still " see " the shepherd out in the wilderness looking for the lost sheep, the woman sweeping the house for the lost coin, the father running down the road to welcome his lost son. It is not surprising that some of the young men in the Armed Services during recent wars report that in trying to remember portions of the Bible they inevitably found themselves thinking of the parables. This is because Jesus made it possible for men to see truth as well as hear it.

When looking for the meaning of a parable, it is essential to remember that a parable is intended to teach one truth and one truth only. By placing that one central idea in a setting that is familiar and striking, it makes the truth unforgettable. Those persons who draw a wide variety of meanings out of each parable are departing sharply from the intention of Jesus. It should also be pointed out that the one truth that a parable is intended to convey is ordinarily a self-evident truth. Modern followers of Jesus, wrestling with the meaning of the parables, may doubt this, but the more we learn of first-century life in Palestine, the more we are struck by the self-evident nature of the truth that the parables convey.

There is one passage, it is true, that states that the purpose of a parable is to conceal the truth rather than make it plain. " To you has been given the secret of the kingdom of God, but for those outside everything is in parables; so that they may indeed see but not perceive, and may indeed hear but not understand; lest they should turn again, and be forgiven." (Mark 4:11-12.) This is a troubling passage on the surface, but many scholars believe that the Greek word translated " so that " has been mistranslated and should read " because." Thus Jesus used parables *because* those on the outside need simple, direct teaching. Other scholars believe that this passage comes from a later writer who was attempting to explain why the Jews as a whole rejected the gospel. How was it possible that the teaching of Jesus was misunderstood and rejected by so many? The theory that Jesus used the parable to conceal his thoughts provides an answer to that question. He was not understood because it was God's plan for him to be misunderstood and crucified. It should be noted that some such explanation for this passage is necessary because Jesus obviously used the parables to reveal more and more of the " secrets " of the Kingdom to all men (Matt. 13:1-17; Luke 8:9). His main purpose was to bring the message of God straight to the minds and hearts of men. He taught in parables because parables conveyed God's truth in a vivid and memorable setting that any man could understand and remember.

Jesus occasionally used the allegory as a technique in teaching, a fact that complicates the picture, since parable and allegory are frequently confused. In contrast with the parable that is intended to convey one truth, the allegory is intended to convey many truths. It is usually a lengthy story in which every detail has symbolic meaning. Augustine weakened the parable of the good Samaritan by turning it into an allegory in which the victim is Adam, the thieves are the devil and his angels, the Samaritan is Christ, the oil is comfort, the inn is the church, the innkeeper is Paul, and on and on. How different the story sounds from the original parable that was intended simply to demonstrate the meaning of " neighborly love "! It should be noted that there are at least forty parables in the Gospels and only two allegories, that of the sower (Mark 4:13-20) and the weeds (Matt. 13:36-43).

Short sayings also played a prominent role in the teaching of Jesus. He often set forth his ideas in brief, clear, memorable, sometimes shocking statements. These were filled with imagery and were short enough to be remembered easily. " No one who puts his hand to the plow and looks back is fit for the kingdom of God." " No one puts new wine into old wineskins." It is probable that the editors of the Gospels have collected many of these short sayings and placed them in longer discourses such as the Sermon on the Mount. The Gospel of Mark, especially, employs the principle of association, grouping certain sayings together around a word or idea that they have in common.

Paradoxes also appear in the teaching of Jesus as an effective means of shocking people's minds into alertness and thus preparing them for the truth. A paradox is simply a statement that appears self-contradictory or opposed to common sense. "Whoever would save his life will lose it; and whoever loses his life for my sake and the gospel's will save it." "The last will be first, and the first last." No one wrestling with the truth in such paradoxes could ever forget them, for they have a haunting quality about them that will not let the mind remain at rest.

Other techniques of teaching employed by Jesus include repetition and antithesis. He would repeat ideas for emphasis, often presenting parables or statements in doublet or triplet. At other times he emphasized the contrast and opposition of the antithesis, a method commonly employed in Hebrew poetry. He also acted out prophetic passages, as the old-time prophets had done, and he occasionally used material objects in teaching, such as bread and wine at the Last Supper. Nor should we overlook the fact that he probably preached sermons and discourses of some length, such as that which preceded the feeding of the five thousand, but many of these have been lost simply because there was no one present to record them verbatim.

In all of these ways, Jesus made the truth real to his hearers. His simple, direct, authoritative approach places him in the company of history's greatest teachers. Important as this is, however, it is not primarily his technique that accounts for the countless transformed lives of those touched by his teaching. It is the content of his message that made the difference, the proclamation of the good news of God.

10

The Nature of God

THE HUNGER for God is the deepest hunger of man's existence. When we try to ignore it, it only becomes more insistent. When we try to satisfy it with the fleeting pleasures of sex, society, or security, the pangs return to haunt us in the night. We may even try to deny it openly, but after our most eloquent argument the hunger remains to prove us wrong. When man is honest with himself he knows that he has been created for companionship with God.

William Blake was trying to say this when he once pictured a small man at the foot of a very tall ladder. Looking up toward heaven, the man wanted to climb, but he was afraid of the dizzy height. All he could do was stand at the foot of the ladder, looking upward, and cry, "I want, I want!" When a man openly stands in this position, expressing his desire for God, he has taken the first step toward the creative fulfillment of his humanity.

Many men in many ages have expressed this basic fact of our human existence. The Chinese philosopher Lao-tzu, who lived six hundred years before Christ, said: "As rivers have their source in some far-off mountain, so the human spirit has its source. To find his fountain of spirit is to learn the secret of heaven and earth." The Old Testament psalmist put it a different way when he cried: "As a hart longs for flowing streams, so longs my soul for thee, O God. My soul thirsts for God, for the living God." Meister Eckhart, a Christian mystic, speaks of seed and growth in expressing his own experience: "The seed of God is in us. Given an intelligent farmer and a diligent field hand, it will thrive and grow up to God, whose seed it is." Another German mystic described a deep inner abyss where God dwells. "Oh, who will give me a voice," he proclaimed, "that I may cry aloud to the whole world that God, the all-highest, is in the deepest abyss within us and is waiting for us to return to him!"

Many others have expressed man's hunger for God in eloquent ways. But no one has fed this hunger as Jesus does in his teaching about God. He placed God at the center and revealed the nature of God more clearly than anyone else who ever lived. Relatedness to God, he insisted, is the one thing needful, the first commandment, the pearl of great price, the treasure hidden in a field. The teaching of Jesus awakens a response in the hearts of men because it is primarily teaching about God. He did not waste time proving the existence of God, nor did he enter into a systematic discussion of the attributes of God. But his clear words, his unforgettable images, and his dramatic example made God more real to men than he had ever been before. The teaching of Jesus begins, continues, and ends in God.

A. Inheritance from Judaism

Many of the central ideas that Jesus developed are taken from the religious structure of Judaism. His words about God sound familiar to readers of the Old Testament because the God he described was essentially revealed in the Jewish Scriptures. He was, as Jesus described him, "the God of Abraham, and the God of Isaac, and the God of Jacob."

Jesus assumed, for example, the existence of one God. Monotheism, one of the supreme gifts of Judaism to the history of mankind, developed over a long period of Old Testament history. There is a good deal of evidence that the Hebrews before the time of Moses were polytheistic. Even while the covenant rela-

earth his footstool (Matt. 5:34). "All things are possible to thee,"
he prayed. (Mark 14:36.) He told his disciples that God had created man, that he made his sun rise and sent the rain, that he fed
the birds and clothed the lilies of the field. "And do not fear
those," he said, "who kill the body but cannot kill the soul;
rather fear him who can destroy both soul and body in hell."
(Matt. 10:28.) Such is the irresistible power of the one true God!

Closely related to the creative power of God is his holiness,
both in the sense of majesty and moral perfection. In the Old
Testament the Hebrews took off their shoes in his presence,
dared not look at him, and feared they would drop dead if they
accidently touched the Ark of the Covenant, which was the symbol of his presence. Few passages in literature better describe
this holiness of God than the sixth chapter of Isaiah, when God's
presence filled the Temple, "and the foundations of the thresh-
old shook at the voice of him who called, and the house was
filled with smoke." The sense of awe was so great among the
Hebrews that they even hesitated to mention the divine name!

One of the amazing things about the teaching of Jesus is the
way in which he combined the ideas of holiness and love in the
being of God. He is a loving Father, as we shall see, eager for his
children to come to him. At the same time, he is the "Holy
Father." Quoting the Old Testament, he said, "You shall worship the Lord your God and him only shall you serve" (Matt.
4:10). When a man called him "Good Teacher," he replied:
"Why do you call me good? No one is good but God alone"
(Mark 10:18). In the model prayer he taught his disciples to
say, "Our Father who art in heaven, hallowed be thy name"
(Matt. 6:9). All of this is a far cry from the blasphemous familiarity that many moderns feel toward God. For many he is
"the man upstairs," or "a real livin' doll," as one Hollywood
star put it. Such an attitude is far removed from the awe and
reverence of the Old Testament and the Gospels where the
mysterium tremendum of God's presence is so pervading.

Finally, the Old Testament emphasizes the uncompromising righteousness of God. With him there is no minimizing of evil, no toleration of wrong. He is unalterably opposed to evil and will destroy it. When Moses broke the tablets of the law he was punished. From the moment of his great sin with Bathsheba the fortunes of David declined. Solomon and the kings of Israel and Judah who followed him were all punished for following other gods. One line from *The Green Pastures* captures the Old Testament spirit beautifully when God says, " When you anger me, I'm a God of wrath! "

The forgiving love of God, which Jesus emphasized, does not minimize the strength of this uncompromising righteousness. Heine, the German poet, demonstrated the shallowness of his faith when he replied to a friend who had tried to comfort him in his dying moment by assuring him of God's forgiveness. Said Heine: " Of course he will forgive. It's his business to forgive! " But it isn't this easy. Jesus spoke of a time of judgment when the evil would be separated from the righteous and thrown into a furnace of fire where men will weep and gnash their teeth (Matt. 13:50). He spoke of the separation of weeds and wheat so that the weeds could be burned (Matt. 13:30). He told of a time when God would say to those at his left hand, "Depart from me, you cursed, into the eternal fire prepared for the devil and his angels " (Matt. 25:41). He took sin very seriously and constantly called men to repentance. The righteousness of God is an ever-present theme in the teaching of Jesus.

In many such aspects of Jesus' teaching, we find evidence of his debt to his Jewish background. He accepted the deep value of the Old Testament revelation of God, yet at the same time we cannot study the teaching of Jesus without feeling that we are out of the Old Testament and in a strange, new world. Jesus himself warned against trying to put new wine into an old wineskin or to sew a new patch on an old garment. His teaching simply would not fit within the framework of the old, for although it reflected the Old Testament heritage, in many ways it was entirely new. This is especially obvious in his teaching about God as Father.

B. The Loving Father

The conception of God as a Father was not entirely new in Judaism. On the contrary, it appears several times in the Prophets and The Psalms. " As a father pities his children, so the Lord pities those who fear him," said the psalmist (Ps. 103:13). In Jeremiah, God says, " For I am a father to Israel, and Ephraim is my first-born." (Jer. 31:9.) In one of the moving chapters of the Old Testament, Hosea pictures God as a loving father helping Israel to learn to walk (Hos., ch. 11). In these and other passages the idea of the Fatherhood of God appears in the Old Testament, but it was never fully developed there. The great emphasis in the Old Testament is upon God as a righteous king. As we have just seen, Jesus did not repudiate the truths in that concept, but his major emphasis was entirely different.

For Jesus, God was a loving Father. Here is the truly unique contribution that he made to man's understanding of the nature of God. He used the term so often and filled it with such meaning that man's conception of God has been different ever since. The Gethsemane prayer begins, " Abba, Father." The great thanksgiving prayer is, " I thank thee, Father." When his disciples ask him to teach them to pray it is the same, " Our Father." Again and again the term is on his lips in parable and prayer. In the four Gospels it appears one hundred and forty-two times! For Jesus, God is the Father.

This means, for one thing, that he is a personal God. Personality is the highest order of being that is known to man. It is not surprising that Jesus implies that God, whatever else he is, is at least the supreme Person. His very nature is to be interpreted in terms of will, consciousness, and love. Some persons mistakenly believe they are expressing greater reverence for God by rejecting the concept of personality and referring to him as " creative process," "the Absolute," or "the Sovereign Other." But this is saying less about God than Jesus said when he called him Father.

Above all, however, when Jesus spoke of the Fatherhood of God he meant to emphasize the love of God. For Jesus, God's very nature is an infinite activity of love. As a father loves his children, willing if necessary to give his life for them, so God loves us. Love is at the heart of the universe, directing its creative process. The meaning of the whole creation and the meaning of man's life are rooted in the divine love. As a little Chinese girl who had just learned about the Christian God said: "Our gods ask so much. Your God gives so much." The truth is that he gives himself as love.

He gives himself, in the first place, as active love. In some religions the divine being is engaged in self-contemplation; in others he is entirely passive. But for Jesus, God is active, outgoing love. God cares! His love moves out to seek the sinner, the lost, the heavy-laden. The Father will not rest until his children have been found. He is pursuing us in love, relentlessly, tirelessly.

When Ann Sullivan first visited Helen Keller, the little girl was living in her dark and silent world in total isolation. No one could do anything with her, but watched her hysterical tantrums in helpless despair. Miss Sullivan, who had come as her teacher, realized that her first task was to "get through" to the child, to establish some means of communication. She therefore took the girl out into the yard, ran cold well water over her hand, and then wrote "w-a-t-e-r" across the palm of her hand. Then she repeated the process, again and again, day after day, week after week. Patiently, lovingly, she kept this up until one day the little girl suddenly took her teacher's hand, ran water over it and wrote, slowly and painfully, "w-a-t-e-r." Ann Sullivan said it was one of the happiest moments in her life, for she knew that at long last she had succeeded in getting through.

With infinitely greater patience and love, God is trying to get through to us. Jesus said God is like a shepherd who knows each time one sheep is lost, and is always eager to go out into the night, searching until he finds it (Luke 15:3-7). He is like a poor woman who has lost a coin and cannot rest until she has "turned the house upside down" to find it (Luke 15:8-10). As a loving Father, he gives good gifts to his children, indeed, "it is your Father's good pleasure to give you the kingdom" (Luke 12:32). It is his good pleasure to give because it is his nature to love, actively and tirelessly.

His love is also unlimited. It is infinite, extending to the lowest and least of his creation. No one is beyond the circle of his concern. Every individual has a unique and personal value in his sight. This idea is one of the greatest contributions ever made to the religious and moral thought of the world, for it lays the foundation for social progress, the rights of individuals, and the responsibility of men for one another. Immanuel Kant was simply reflecting what Jesus had implied long before when he said that we should never look upon persons as means to an end but always as ends in themselves.

Jesus emphasized this unlimited loving concern of God when he said that God's love extends even to the sparrows, the cheapest article of food on the market. "Are not two sparrows sold for a penny?" he asked. "And not one of them will fall to the ground without your Father's will." (Matt. 10:29-30.) In Matthew's version of the parable of the lost sheep, Jesus says, "It is not the will of my Father who is in heaven that one of these little ones should perish" (Matt. 18:10-14). "Even the hairs of your head are all numbered." (Matt. 10:30.)

Finally, Jesus insisted that the Father's love is merciful or forgiving love. He is eager to forgive, to give another chance to those who have gone wrong. He judges sin, but as the loving Father, he is eager to forgive the sinner who repents. In one of the greatest stories ever told, he related the sad experience of a boy who took his inheritance and went off to a far country. There he wasted his living, and finally "came to himself," returning home in fear and repentance. Imagine his amazement when he saw his father running down the road to greet and forgive him. (Luke 15:11-32.) The second part of this same parable is a severe rebuke to those who criticize this attitude of forgiving love. We should note also the number of times Jesus urged men to forgive others so that they might know what it means to be forgiven by God (cf. Matt. 6:14-15) and the number of times he spoke of how men are forgiven when they turn to God in humble repentance (cf. Luke 18:13).

Something of the meaning of God's active, unlimited, forgiving love was caught in a newspaper account of a little girl lost in the woods during a family camping trip. Her father, in desperation, looked for her in the nearby stream and through the forest. Finally one of the other searchers found her and brought her safely back to her anxious parents. That night when her father had tucked her in bed, she hugged him and said, "Daddy, aren't you glad you found me!" Only a father who has found a lost child could know this father's joy in having her safely home. But Jesus said that God is like this. Tirelessly, patiently, he searches for us until he finds us. And when he finds us, said Jesus, "there is joy before the angels of God," and "joy in heaven."

God is a loving Father. This concept, fully developed, brings man to the pinnacle of his experience of God. The center of Jesus' life and teaching is his own experience of this divine love.

C. The Reality of God

One summer in New Hampshire, I unwittingly enacted a parable of man's dilemma in his relationship to God. We were staying in a little cottage on Lake Winnepesaukee when I decided to take an early morning hike up a nearby mountain. Climbing was difficult, since the slope was almost perpendicular. For nearly an hour I struggled upward, head down, pulling myself along from rock to rock and from tree to tree. Finally, needing a rest, I turned around and almost lost my footing because the beauty of the view literally staggered me. I had climbed high enough to see nearly the whole of the lake, azure-blue lying in its emerald-green setting, and I knew then why the Indians had named it Winnepesaukee, "the smile of the Great Spirit." But I also realized that I had almost missed this unforgettable scene. It was at my back all the while, but struggling upward, step by step, I had no time to enjoy it.

How often I have remembered this moment when talking to others who are struggling upward each day from problem to problem with no time to stop and enjoy the smile of the "Great Spirit"! Because of this hectic kind of feverish existence, God remains for many, at best, abstract and external. He is an object of thought, occasionally an object of worship. But he loses his reality and his nearness, with the sense of his living presence wholly missing.

One of the truly amazing things about Jesus is the reality of his own experience of God. God is never simply an object of thought or worship. He is directly perceived or "known" in the inner experience of Jesus. God is consciously present in every moment of his life, no abstract concept, but an immediate and living reality. He does not speak of God as he has conceived him but as he has felt him, seen him, experienced him, known him.

In a few rare personalities something of this same awareness shines forth. Augustine, for example, in his *Confessions,* utters the passionate cry: "Too late love I thee, O thou Beauty of ancient days, yet ever new! Behold, thou wert within and I abroad, and there I searched for thee. Thou wert with me, but I was not with thee." But such an awareness is rare, and in no one else does it approach the intensity exhibited by Jesus. His life grows out of his living experience of God. His filial consciousness is a direct consciousness within his own inner being. His obedience to the will of God is faithful and loving obedience to a Father whom he has known. This sense of the reality of God is one of the facets of the Gospel records which makes the life of Jesus utterly unique and gives his teaching an authority unknown among the sons of men.

Emily Dickinson once spoke of the "hazy oblong blur which my parents worship and call God." For all too many people, God is a hazy oblong blur. It was the unique contribution of Jesus to bring this hazy oblong blur into sharp focus, revealing the reality of God as a loving Father.

11

The Nature of the Kingdom

THE KINGDOM (reign) of God is the central theme of the life and teaching of Jesus. It was the theme of his first sermon as reported by Mark: "The time is fulfilled, and the kingdom of God is at hand; repent, and believe in the gospel" (Mark 1:15). On the last night of his life, before he led the disciples out into the Garden, he referred confidently to the Kingdom: "Truly, I say to you, I shall not drink again of the fruit of the vine until that day when I drink it new in the kingdom of God" (Mark 14:25). Between these two extremities of his public ministry the phrase is constantly on his lips. Nearly all the parables begin, "The kingdom of God is like. . ." Sometimes he talks about God and the Kingdom, sometimes about man and the Kingdom, sometimes about himself and the Kingdom, but the Kingdom is always the common point of reference. He was a man of deep compassion and spent a good deal of time healing the sick, but he would not let even his healing ministry interfere with the proclamation of the Kingdom. He told others to seek first the Kingdom of God, and he did this himself in every incident of his life and in every word of his teaching. We cannot hope to understand his message until we gain some comprehension of the nature of the Kingdom.

A. Significance of the Kingdom

Jesus was certain that the Kingdom was the most important thing in life. Here man discovers the reason for his birth, the purpose for his life, the hope for his future. This is the treasure hidden in a field, so desirable that when a man finds it he sells all that he has to buy the field. (Matt. 13:44.) It is the pearl of great price, so valuable that a merchant upon finding it will sell everything to buy it. (Matt. 13:45.) When he was in the home of Martha and Mary, Jesus told them that Mary, in taking time to find out about the Kingdom, had found the " one thing needful." (Luke 10:38-42.) He told all of his followers to seek *first* the Kingdom. (Matt. 6:33.) The Kingdom is in fact so important that it is better to cut off a hand or foot than to miss it. (Mark 9:42-48.)

The note of urgency that he sounded so often underlines the significance of the Kingdom in his thought. In his first sermon he emphasized the fact that the Kingdom " is at hand," and " the time is fulfilled." When he sent the disciples out on their preaching mission he gave them emergency instructions and told them they would see greater evidence of the presence of God's Kingdom upon their return. (Matt. 10:17-23.) On another occasion he said to a gathered crowd, " There are some standing here who will not taste death before they see the kingdom of God come with power " (Mark 9:1). This atmosphere of urgency naturally heightened the excitement among his followers as they listened to him teach.

It is hard for many modern followers of Jesus to appreciate fully this emphasis which Jesus placed upon the Kingdom. There are so many other tempting purposes for life beckoning for time and loyalty that we fail to appreciate how Jesus placed this at the top of the scale of values as the " one thing needful." Some years ago in New England, I attended a marathon race, which had a bizarre ending. All had gone well for several miles, but sud-

denly the runners came to an unmarked fork in the road. Looking around in confusion, they followed the advice of two small
boys sitting on the fence who pointed off to the right. After a
while they discovered they were on a dead-end road, but by this
time there was so much confusion the officials decided to call off
the race. When they went back to the unmarked fork they found
that the two little boys had long since departed, but not before
replacing the markers that would have directed the runners to
the opposite fork and the open road. Modern society is full of
people sitting on the fence, trying to direct others down the
wrong roads. Jesus, on the other hand, made it perfectly clear
that there is only one open road, one purpose for life. All others
lead to a dead-end of despair. He gave his life and devoted his
teaching to the task of helping men find the open road to God
and thus fulfill the supreme purpose of their lives.

B. Definition of the Kingdom

New Testament readers often find it confusing to discover
several terms used to express the idea of the Kingdom. Usually
it is called " the kingdom of God," but Matthew consistently refers to it as " the kingdom of heaven." In other places it is " the
kingdom of the Son of man," " the kingdom of Christ," or " my
Father's kingdom." It is therefore necessary to realize that all of
these expressions refer to the same basic concept. Matthew, for
example, in good Jewish fashion, simply substituted the word
" heaven " in an attempt to avoid the use of the divine name.
Since the Kingdom is the subject of so much New Testament
writing, it is not surprising that different expressions have been
used in reference to it.

Somewhat more confusing is the fact that the Hebrew word
malkuth and the Greek word *basileia* do not ordinarily mean
" kingdom " in our English usage. There are really three different ways in which the term is employed in the Gospels. It may

mean (1) kingly rule of God, (2) the subjects ruled, or (3) the realm or sphere of the rule.

The first meaning is the basic one, for the word is ordinarily used to refer to the ruling activity of God. In the phrase "kingly rule of God," the emphasis is upon "God" and "rule," not upon "kingly" as it seems in the usual English rendition. Although the Revised Standard Version of the Bible prefers to follow the traditional usage, students of the life and teaching of Jesus will find it helpful to substitute the phrase "kingly rule of God," or "rule of God," or "reign of God" in many of the sayings of Jesus. This practice has been adopted in many recent books in the field.

Since a king can scarcely rule without subjects, however, the people who are "the ruled" are occasionally spoken of as "the kingdom." There are some parables whose meaning remains obscure until the phrase "the subjects who are ruled" is substituted for the English "kingdom of God."

Further, since a reign or rule does not operate in a void, the phrase may also refer to the realm or sphere of God's rule, including both king and subjects. It should be noted that our English word "kingdom" conveys only this third meaning.

Carl Sandburg tells a delightful story about a college boy who took a fraternity brother named Specknoodle home and tried to introduce him to his deaf grandmother. After several unsuccessful attempts to understand she said: "It's no use. No matter how you say it, it still sounds like Specknoodle to me." A first reading may give the impression that no matter how we say it, kingdom still sounds like "kingdom." But the different shades of meaning suggested above are actually of very great importance, and the substitution of one or the other may unlock a parable or saying that otherwise remains a baffling mystery.

C. The Nature of the Kingdom

We have already seen how deeply the religious heritage of
Jesus was rooted in the religion of the Old Testament. This is
nowhere seen more clearly than in his teaching concerning the
nature of the Kingdom. The kingly rule of God was at the
heart of the Hebrew religion from the very earliest times and
reached its highest expression in the message of the great
prophets. Strangely enough, however, Jesus and his contemporaries, both developing their teaching out of this Old Testament
heritage, arrived at very different conclusions. This situation, so
obvious in the Gospel narratives, may be summarized as follows:

THE RULE OF GOD

CONTEMPORARIES OF JESUS
1. God's initiative (yes)
2. National power (emphasized!)
3. Material blessings (emphasized!)
4. Messiah as agent (worldly hero)
5. Religious aspect (generally ignored)
6. Eschatology (apocalypticism)

OLD TESTAMENT PROPHETS
1. God's initiative
2. National power
3. Material blessings
4. Messiah as agent
5. Religious aspect
6. Eschatology

JESUS
1. God's initiative (yes)
2. National power (denied)
3. Material blessings (denied)
4. Messiah as agent (Suffering Servant)
5. Religious aspect (emphasized!)
6. Eschatology (?)

In this chart we may trace the development of six important
aspects of the Kingdom of God from the Old Testament into
the thought of Jesus and his contemporaries. In doing so, we see

quite clearly the striking departure of Jesus from the trend of his own time.

The Old Testament Prophets

According to the great prophets of Israel, the kingly rule of God would be established on the initiative of God. It is not something man can " build " or " create " in any way. Again and again they speak of the " day of the Lord " when God will establish his reign. " The Lord will go forth . . . ," says Zechariah, " and the Lord will become king over all the earth; on that day the Lord will be one and his name one." (Zech. 14:3, 9.) " For the day of the Lord is near upon all the nations. . . . And the kingdom shall be the Lord's." (Obad. 15 and 21.) Belief in the divine initiative is present in all of the prophetic writing.

The great prophets also realized that the initiation of God's rule would mean national vindication and reward for Israel. The scattered tribes would be gathered, Israel's enemies would be destroyed, and all nations would recognize Zion as the center of world rule. Many of the prophets believed that Israel would be punished first for her wickedness, but after punishment would come vindication. Deutero-Isaiah expressed this hope eloquently: " Break forth together into singing, you waste places of Jerusalem; for the Lord has comforted his people, he has redeemed Jerusalem. The Lord has bared his holy arm before the eyes of all the nations; and all the ends of the earth shall see the salvation of our God " (Isa. 52:9-10). " They shall come," said Jeremiah, " and sing aloud on the height of Zion, and they shall be radiant over the goodness of the Lord." (Jer. 31:12.) And Isaiah of Jerusalem speaks of the time when " it shall come to pass in the latter days that the mountain of the house of the Lord shall be established as the highest of the mountains, and shall be raised above the hills; and all the nations shall flow to it. . . . For out of Zion shall go forth the law, and the word of the Lord from Jerusalem " (Isa. 2:2-3).

Along with national vindication will come material blessings. The coming of the reign of God will be the beginning of a golden age of peace and plenty for all. Few passages in the Bible surpass the beauty of the prophetic description of the prosperity to come. Amos writes of the days that are coming "when the plowman shall overtake the reaper and the treader of grapes him who sows the seed; the mountain shall drip sweet wine, and all the hills shall flow with it" (Amos 9:13). Isaiah also speaks of such a time: "The wilderness and the dry land shall be glad, the desert shall rejoice and blossom; like the crocus it shall blossom abundantly, and rejoice with joy and singing" (Isa. 35:1-2).

The concept of the Messiah has a long and varied history, but the idea of an "anointed one" who would act as God's agent in the establishment of the Kingdom became increasingly prominent in the thought of Judaism. There is little agreement on the description of the Messiah, but most men thought in terms of a Davidic ruler who would restore the glory of Israel. Many passages from the prophets were quickly associated with the growing Messianic expectations. "There shall come forth a shoot from the stump of Jesse," wrote Isaiah, "and a branch shall grow out of his roots. And the Spirit of the Lord shall rest upon him, the spirit of wisdom and understanding, the spirit of counsel and might, the spirit of knowledge and the fear of the Lord." (Isa. 11:1-2.) When Jesus rode into Jerusalem, as we have seen, he consciously chose a Messianic prophecy from Zechariah: "Rejoice greatly, O daughter of Zion! Shout aloud, O daughter of Jerusalem! Lo, your king comes to you" (Zech. 9:9). Malachi speaks of the time when "the Lord whom you seek will suddenly come to his temple; the messenger of the covenant in whom you delight. . . . But who can endure the day of his coming, and who can stand when he appears?" (Mal. 3:1-2).

The great prophets also believed that the rule of God would be characterized by complete obedience to God's will and by consciousness of the divine presence. Though often overlooked by the people, these religious aspects of the reign of God were at the center of the thought of men like Ezekiel, Jeremiah, and Isaiah. In Jeremiah, God speaks of the time when he will put his law within the people and write it upon their hearts. " And no longer shall each man teach his neighbor and each his brother, saying, ' Know the Lord,' for they shall all know me." (Jer. 31:33-34.) " A new heart I will give you, and a new spirit I will put within you. . . . And I will put my spirit within you, and cause you to walk in my statutes and be careful to observe my ordinances." (Ezek. 36:26.) And Isaiah says that in that time " the earth shall be full of the knowledge of the Lord as the waters cover the sea " (Isa. 11:9).

Finally, though the Old Testament prophets emphasized the divine initiative in the establishment of the reign of God, many of them believed that the time was near. God's age-long final purpose was about to be fulfilled. Eschatology, speculation about the end-time, was a prominent feature of their writing. " Blow the trumpet in Zion; sound the alarm on my holy mountain! Let all the inhabitants of the land tremble, for the day of the Lord is coming, it is near! " (Joel 2:1-2.) " Be silent before the Lord God! For the day of the Lord is at hand. . . . The great day of the Lord is near, near and hastening fast." (Zeph. 1:7, 14.) Ordinarily these prophets did not attempt to define the end-time in great detail, but many were convinced that the end was imminent.

The Contemporaries of Jesus

First-century Jewish thought concerning the Kingdom of God is clearly seen by comparing it with the prophetic ideas mentioned above.

In general, the people followed the prophetic belief that the rule of God would be established at the initiative of God. Since he was sovereign over all of his creation, he would choose the time to express this sovereignty in terms of a visible reign on earth. The Zealots were the notable exception to this view, in-

sisting that the reign of God could be hastened through revolutionary activity. Apparently they represented a small minority
of the Jews at the time of Jesus, but they were vocal in expressing
their revolutionary doctrine and they constantly fanned the
smoldering unrest of the people. As Jewish patriots, they were
courageous men, but many of their expectations concerning the
coming of the reign of God stood outside the main stream of
Jewish thought.

The idea of national vindication that had been expressed by
the prophets had become a major emphasis by the time of Jesus.
This was the thing the people thought most about in connection
with the idea of the Kingdom. In Esdras, for example, one of the
prominent Jewish books of the time, the peaceful multitude, gathered after the Messiah's annihilation of the Lord's enemies, is
made up of the ten tribes of Israel that had been carried into
exile. One of the most common synagogue prayers of the time
expressed the same feeling: "Blessed art thou, O Lord, who
gatherest the dispersed of his people Israel." In view of the continuously oppressive domination of Israel by foreign powers, now
worse than ever under Rome, it is not surprising that nationalistic aspirations loomed so large in speculation concerning the
end-time.

Almost as important, especially in the minds of the populace,
was the prophetic promise of material blessing that would ac-
company God's rule. This also is not surprising in view of the
very desperate economic conditions of the time. Many of the passages in the contemporary literature match the older prophetic
descriptions of the marvelous productiveness of the land. "The
earth will yield her fruits ten thousand fold," says the Syriac
Baruch. "On one vine will be a thousand clusters, each cluster
of a thousand grapes, and each grape will yield a *kor* [about
ninety gallons] of wine." It should be noted also in this connection that Messianic banquet scenes where all would be richly
fed continued to be a prominent feature of contemporary thought.

Like the prophets of the Old Testament, the contemporaries of Jesus believed in the Messiah as the agent who would establish God's kingly rule. They pictured him largely as a national hero in the Davidic tradition, a leader with great political and military skill. These expectations are well illustrated by a certain Bar-Cochba, "the star man," a revolutionary leader who initiated a political uprising about a century after Jesus. Many of the Jews were certain that he was the Messiah, becoming disillusioned only after a costly three-year war. Still, they were convinced that the Messiah, the "one to come," would be just such a man.

It would not be fair to say that the religious aspects of the rule of God were entirely ignored by the contemporaries of Jesus. Great teachers such as Shammai and Hillel labored to apply the religious traditions of the past to the needs of the present. But for the most part, man's obedience to the will of God was not a prominent feature of current expectations. Political tension, economic suffering, and other factors of everyday life militated against any consuming interest in the deeper issues of life. An independent homeland, a full table, and a great leader whom they could follow — these were the things of which their dreams were made.

Finally, they developed an extreme form of eschatological hope called apocalypticism, from a word meaning "to uncover." This term is applied to all attempts to uncover or reveal the details of the end-time or the end of history. To say that speculation concerning the rule of God among the contemporaries of Jesus was apocalyptic is to put it mildly. Both leaders and people were caught up in endless discussions concerning the ways in which the end would come and in endless predictions of when it would come. The Book of Enoch, widely read during this time, is a typical example. In one place the writer describes how the stars, the fallen angels, and the blinded sheep (unfaithful Jews) will be brought before the throne of God, convicted, and cast into abysses of fire just before the beginning of the golden age. In view of the wide popular appeal of this type of thought, it is not difficult to see why Jesus experienced incredible difficulty in promulgating his own interpretation of the kingly rule of God.

Jesus

In nearly every respect, Jesus stood in direct opposition to the thought of his contemporaries on this all-important subject. Even a perfunctory reading of the Gospels makes it quite clear why Jesus was crucified only a few short months after his announcement to the astonished Galileans that the rule of God was at hand. Their hopes rose to new heights of expectation, only to be shattered by his interpretation of what the kingly rule of God would mean. As the weeks passed, they became certain that any man with such ideas must be a false Messiah!

The emphasis on God's initiative in establishing the Kingdom was the one place of general agreement. He agreed with the Old Testament prophets and with the majority of his fellow Jews that the rule of God would come as a result of God's own act. "Fear not, little flock," he said, "for it is your Father's good pleasure to give you the kingdom." (Luke 12:32.) He also told a parable about a growing seed, emphasizing the way in which the seed's growth comes from God. In the same way, the growth of the Kingdom will come from God. Jesus called upon men to enter, accept, and live in the Kingdom, but never to build or create it.

He disagreed with his contemporaries, however, when they emphasized national vindication as an aspect of the rule of God. In the wilderness at the beginning of his ministry he had wrestled with the temptation to conquer "the kingdoms of the world" and establish the world rule of his homeland. But he rejected the temptation vigorously, certain that the goal of God's reign was something much higher than mere national power. He also made it clear that the rule of God was intended for all men and not just for the "chosen people." In fact, as opposition grew, Jesus seemed to say that Israel would be rejected and the benefits of the Kingdom given to others. " I tell you, many will come from east and west and sit at table with Abraham, Isaac, and Jacob in the kingdom of heaven, while the sons of the kingdom will be thrown into the outer darkness." (Matt. 8:11.) Thus he kindled fires of anger in the hearts of the nationalistic Zealots!

He also opposed the all too popular dreams of material blessings in the Kingdom that was coming. The first temptation in the wilderness had been the temptation to turn stones into bread, to become the economic Messiah who would fulfill the materialistic desires of his hungry countrymen. But Jesus knew the danger of trying to " live by bread alone," and he went out of his way to warn against reliance on riches. He told his followers that they could not serve two masters, God and mammon. (Matt. 6:24.) In one of the most inescapable verbal thrusts of his ministry he said, " It is easier for a camel to go through the eye of a needle than for a rich man to enter the kingdom of God " (Mark 10:25). An especially descriptive passage in the Sermon on the Mount warns against anxiety over food and clothing (Matt. 6:25-33). In closing this same passage he insisted that men " seek first his kingdom," thus making it quite plain that the Kingdom of God did not consist in eating and material comfort.

We have already emphasized the fact that Jesus was certain of his own role as Messiah, but that he was not the Messiah most everyone was expecting. He agreed with those prophets who had insisted that God would send his own Messiah, his " anointed one," to initiate his rule. He disagreed with his contemporaries who interpreted this in terms of secular, military, political power. He had rejected this temptation in the wilderness when he considered the possibility of using his power to perform dazzling miracles, such as throwing himself down from the pinnacle of the Temple. The deepest meaning of his Messianic ministry would be expressed, not in the role of worldly hero, but in the role of Suffering Servant. The application of the Suffering Servant passages of Isaiah to the Messiah was new in Judaism, even shocking, as we see from the reaction of his own disciples. The idea that his friends found most difficult to accept and that his enemies would not accept at all was the idea of a Messiah who would suffer and die.

What Jesus did emphasize in his teaching was the very thing that his contemporaries had largely ignored, the religious aspects of the rule of God. God's kingly rule over the hearts of men was his major concern. For Jesus, man's problem was not the tyranny of Rome or physical hunger. It was separation from God, the supreme tragedy of any man's existence. He therefore did not talk about political freedom or bread but about reconciliation with God and about the new life with God that followed reconciliation. He spoke about God's will, God's love, God's fatherly goodness, God's forgiveness; about man's need for repentance and faith; about love, humility, sincerity, compassion, and singleness of purpose. Every saying and parable illuminates some aspect of God's purpose, man's relationship to God, or man's relationship to his fellow men in the Kingdom of God. The very aspects of the prophetic writings that his contemporaries rejected became for Jesus the building material out of which he created the structure of his message. God's kingly rule over the hearts of men was the burden of his teaching.

What did Jesus believe about the end-time? Did he predict that the kingly rule of God was near? Since the problem of eschatology in the Gospels is one of the most perplexing in New Testament study, we have set aside the following chapter to discuss the complex issues that are involved.

At this point it is important to see how radically the teaching of Jesus differed from that of his contemporaries. In describing the nature of the Kingdom, they both started at the same place but arrived at destinations that were poles apart. The national vindication and material blessedness that were so prominent in the first-century speculation were of minor significance to Jesus. Their expectation of a worldly hero Messiah was totally rejected in favor of a Suffering Servant Messiah. The religious aspects of the rule of God that they had largely ignored — God's loving will and man's joyful obedience — became for Jesus the true riches of the Kingdom. The clash aroused by these opposing views of the Kingdom is mirrored on every page of the Gospels and largely accounts for the tragic early death of Jesus at the hands of his enemies.

In spite of the obvious dangers involved, Jesus continued to preach the good news of God's rule as it had been revealed to him by the Father. Even if men rejected him, loving and joyful obedience to the will of God was still the pearl of great price. It has been reported that Bernard of Clairvaux placed a sign above the doorway of his small room in the monastery so that he would have to see it whenever he entered. The sign read, " Bernard, why are you here? " Sooner or later every man asks himself that question as he wrestles with the purpose of life. For Jesus, there was only one answer. The kingly rule of God was the one thing needful.

12

The Coming of the Kingdom

WHEN the pilot of the United States Air Force plane that dropped the atomic bomb on Hiroshima in August of 1945 circled back after the bombing run to see what damage had been done, he could not believe his eyes. The entire city had virtually disappeared! Emotionally shaken by the experience, he turned and wrote in the official flight log, "My God, what have we done!"

Many prophets of doom would reply, "You have released the force that will destroy the world!" Such persons are certain that the opening of the atomic era was the beginning of the end. Man now has the power to destroy himself without the moral strength to control that power. For this reason we are told with increasing fervency and frequency that "man's long dialogue on earth is over," that we are now in "the twilight of civilization." Many are the voices of despair, predicting the imminent end of the world.

These predictions have a strange ring of familiarity about them. In every age man has been expecting the end of history. The only difference is that we are now blaming it on man rather than God. Prior to the modern era, men just as confidently predicted the end of the world, but they expected it to come as a mighty act of God. The God who had created the world and placed man upon it would at a time of his own choosing destroy his handiwork in a great cosmic cataclysm. Eschatology, literally meaning the "last things," is the name given to speculation concerning this end-time. Apocalypticism refers to the detailed prediction of the time and manner of the last things. Every age produces its own form of apocalypticism. Perhaps the most familiar examples to readers of the Bible are the books of Daniel and Revelation. The writers of both were certain that the end was coming soon.

In view of this persistent human preoccupation with the end of history, it is not surprising to discover that the issue of eschatology is the most perplexing problem of New Testament study. It recurs in nearly every one of the New Testament writings, and is especially troubling in the Gospels. Every Christian is anxious to know what Jesus taught about the end-time, but this is just the problem! Often he seemed to say that the time was fulfilled and the end would come in the near future. On some occasions he spoke as if the kingly rule of God had already come, whereas in other sayings he warns against speculating about the future. The most learned and devout scholars differ radically in assessing the relative value of the Gospel records, so that the average reader may feel hopelessly confused.

What are we to believe about Jesus' teaching concerning the coming of the Kingdom? Would its coming mean the end of history or has it already come? Even more important, is it coming soon?

A. PRESENT VS. FUTURE

There are sayings of Jesus' that make it quite clear that the kingly rule of God is already accomplished. It is present, in our midst. Other sayings imply that it is a thing of the future. Hence the difficulty of determining the true intention of Jesus.

In many short sayings, the kingly rule of God is a present spiritual reality. The poor in spirit and those persecuted for righteousness' sake are called blessed because "theirs is the kingdom of heaven." The disciples have already been given the secrets of the Kingdom. The children are welcomed by Jesus, "for to such belongs the kingdom of heaven." One prominent scholar has estimated that of twenty-seven references to the Kingdom in the primary sources, no less than eighteen imply that it is already present.

Two other statements of Jesus' put the matter more directly. In the Beelzebul controversy, Jesus was accused by his enemies of being able to heal the demon possessed only because he was in league with the prince of demons. Jesus defended himself by pointing out that if his power came from Satan, then Satan was destroying his own house. "But," he said, "if it is by the finger of God that I cast out demons, then the kingdom of God has come upon you." (Luke 11:20.) The present tense is especially striking here, since Jesus obviously believed that his power did come from God. On other occasions, when talking about John the Baptist, Jesus says that the Kingdom has come: "I tell you, among those born of women none is greater than John; yet he who is least in the kingdom of God is greater than he" (Luke 7:28). "The law and the prophets were until John; since then the good news of the kingdom of God is preached, and every one enters it violently." (Luke 16:16.)

Probably the most frequently quoted passage in this connection came out of a conversation with the Pharisees. They had asked him directly about the coming of the Kingdom, and he replied, "The kingdom of God is not coming with signs to be observed; nor will they say, 'Lo, here it is!' or 'There!' for behold, the kingdom of God is in the midst of you" (Luke 17:20-21). There is some question about the correct translation of the last phrase, some commentators insisting it should read, "within you." But in either case, whether in our midst or within, the kingly rule of God is present.

This impressive array of passages can be matched by those in which the Kingdom is obviously yet to come, including the central petition of the Lord's Prayer: "Thy kingdom come, thy will be done" (Matt. 6:10). Many other sayings indicate that entrance into the Kingdom will be a future event: "Not every one who says to me, 'Lord, Lord,' shall enter the kingdom of heaven, but he who does the will of my Father who is in heaven" (Matt. 7:21). "How hard it will be for those who have riches to enter the kingdom of God!" (Mark 10:23.)

On one occasion when Jesus was preaching to the multitude, he said, "Truly, I say to you, there are some standing here who will not taste death before they see the kingdom of God come with power" (Mark 9:1). At another time he was giving the disciples instructions and warning of the dangers they would face. Then he concluded, "Truly, I say to you, you will not have gone through all the towns of Israel, before the Son of man comes." (Matt. 10:23.) These passages are troubling, as we shall see, not only because they imply that the Kingdom is a future reality but also because they predict its imminent coming.

Finally, there is one entire chapter in each of the Synoptic Gospels that is thoroughly apocalyptic, predicting how and when the Kingdom will come (Matt., ch. 24; Mark, ch. 13; Luke, ch. 21). Here it is definitely a future material reality. These chapters, commonly called "the Synoptic apocalypse," are presented as the teaching of Jesus, even though they stand in marked contrast to the spirit of many of his other sayings.

There are three commonly accepted theories that have been proposed to account for the apparent contradiction in these records. Some believe that Jesus preached the Kingdom of God as present, already fully realized in his own life and ministry. This view is known as "realized eschatology," for the end-time is here. The kingly rule of God has been accomplished, not through some future catastrophic event, but in the person of Jesus. The final triumph of God comes through the gradual transformation of humanity, but the real message of Jesus was that divine intervention was no longer a future hope. It was now accomplished in a real and decisive sense through Jesus. C. H. Dodd, the outstanding British scholar who coined the phrase

"realized eschatology," has been joined by many reputable interpreters in defending this position.

At the opposite extreme is the theory known as "thorough-
going eschatology." According to this view, the major emphasis
of Jesus was upon the future reality of God's rule. By an act of
his will, God will replace the present state of sinfulness and misery by a world of righteousness and joy. This will be accomplished through an event of catastrophic proportions and not
through gradual development. No less a scholar than Albert
Schweitzer is convinced that Jesus actually expected this event to
occur before his disciples returned from their tour of Galilee.
When this failed to happen, he revised his strategy and went to
Jerusalem with the deliberate intention of being killed in order
to bring in the Kingdom. Since the crucifixion did not initiate
the catastrophic event, Jesus was obviously in error. Schweitzer
and others further maintain that the ethical teaching of Jesus is
simply an "interim ethic," intended only for the brief interim
before the Kingdom comes. Many of these scholars have an un-
canny way of interpreting all the sayings of Jesus to fit their
conclusion. For example, Luke 17:21 becomes "The kingdom of
God is (all at once) in your midst."

A mediating position between these two extremes is now the
most commonly held view. Actually there is no essential contradiction between these two types of sayings in the teaching of
Jesus. Wherever and whenever an individual or group accepts
and lives in obedience to the will of God, then the Kingdom is
present. Any person can take upon himself the yoke of the Kingdom now that it has been revealed. Thus the Kingdom was present in Jesus, and it was "in the midst" of those who followed
him. In a very real sense, the Kingdom was and is a present
reality.

At the same time it is a definite future reality. One of the most
exciting results of modern New Testament scholarship has been
the emphasis on the eschatological framework of Jesus' teaching.

It is almost impossible to escape the conclusion that he definitely looked forward to some future consummation of the Kingdom, probably as a catastrophic divine event. Goguel, the great French scholar, has skillfully shown how the central thrust of Jesus' message fits well within the bounds of this eschatological expectation. Neither extreme in Jesus' teaching can be interpreted away since there are elements of truth in both.

The fact that the Kingdom is present (in Jesus and in those who accept God's will) and future (in a catastrophic consummation) is suggested by the parables of growth, such as the mustard seed (Mark 4:30-32) and the leaven (Matt. 13:33). The major point here, the contrast between the small beginning and the large harvest, implies that something is definitely present now that will be great in the future.

Thus the general problem of eschatology in the teaching of Jesus is not so great as it appears on the surface. Jesus taught that the Kingdom is both present and future because he believed that God, in his goodness, had already partially established his kingly rule and would in his own good time establish it fully.

B. APOCALYPTICISM VS. WATCHFULNESS

Unfortunately, the problem of apocalypticism is not so easily resolved. Did Jesus predict in detail how the end would come and did he actually expect the end during his own lifetime? Those who answer in the affirmative must be prepared to explain why Jesus was so mistaken on this important issue. Those who answer in the negative, on the other hand, must be prepared to explain the apocalyptic sayings in the Gospels.

When Jesus tried to prepare his disciples for the suffering ahead, he added a note of urgency by predicting that before they had returned from their preaching mission, the Son of man would come (Matt. 10:23). The coming of the Son of man, the heavenly Messiah, to herald the beginning of the new age was a common expectation among first-century Jews. If the saying is genuine, it means that Jesus definitely expected the end of history and the beginning of the new age very soon.

Similarly, his statement to the gathered crowd means that he expected the Kingdom to come in full glory within a generation: "There are some standing here who will not taste death before they see the kingdom of God come with power" (Mark 9:1). Many scholars emphasize this passage as one that proves beyond doubt that Jesus expected the end of the age within a relatively short period.

The greatest difficulty is caused, however, by the apocalyptic chapters in the Synoptic Gospels (Matt., ch. 24; Mark, ch. 13; Luke, ch. 21). In this discourse, Jesus predicts in vivid detail the imminent end of history. The whole thing is cast in the esoteric style common to apocalypticism. There will be earthquakes and famines, brother will deliver up brother to death, the sun will be darkened, the moon will not give its light, and the stars will be falling from heaven. "And then they will see the Son of man coming in clouds with great power and glory. And then he will send out the angels, and gather his elect from the four winds, from the ends of the earth to the ends of heaven." (Mark 13:26-27.) The passage ends with this clear prediction of the impending end: "Truly, I say to you, this generation will not pass away before all these things take place" (Mark 13:30). If this passage is genuine, then the teaching of Jesus was in complete accord with the apocalyptic hopes of his generation.

But can these passages be authentic when there are so many others in which Jesus definitely disclaims any special knowledge of the exact scheme of events that will precede the end-time? When the Pharisees and Sadducees asked him about the signs of the end he replied with unexpected severity, "An evil and adulterous generation seeks for a sign, but no sign shall be given to it except the sign of Jonah" (Matt. 16:4). He warned other Pharisees that "the kingdom of God is not coming with signs to be observed" (Luke 17:20).

Strangely enough, the apocalyptic chapters in the Synoptics all contain sayings of Jesus' in which he denies knowledge of when the end will come, urging men to be watchful. " But of that day or that hour no one knows, not even the angels in heaven, nor the Son, but only the Father. Take heed, watch; for you do not know when the time will come." (Mark 13:32-33.) Matthew's record of this apocalyptic discourse includes a whole series of sayings and parables emphasizing the importance of expectant watchfulness. The parables of the watchful householder, the faithful servant, and the foolish maidens follow one another in rapid succession, thus driving the point home with unusual effectiveness.

How can we account for the contradictory nature of our Gospel records in this matter? Either Jesus confidently predicted the nature and time of the end, or he disclaimed any such knowledge, exhorting his followers to watchfulness because no one knows when the end will be. In an attempt to resolve this problem, scholars have usually accepted one of three possible explanations.

Goguel believes that the thinking of Jesus on this subject changed as his ministry developed, passing through three definite phases. When he sent out the disciples, he believed that the end was very near. A little later, he revised this idea, stating that the end would come within a generation. At the last he simply spoke in terms of watchfulness, uncertain about the definite signs of the end. This theory accounts for the contradictory nature of the sources, but it is based on sheer speculation. There is no evidence in the Gospels to indicate any such development in his thought. On the contrary, many of the apocalyptic passages occur at the end of his ministry rather than at the beginning. Goguel's theory has won acceptance from some reputable scholars, but it directly contradicts the Gospel tradition as handed down to us in the Synoptics.

An increasing number of scholars are now accepting another alternative, namely, that Jesus was in error in this phase of his teaching. Many of these men insist that Jesus was a man of his age in many ways, especially in viewing the end of history in fore-shortened perspective. Like his contemporaries, he believed that the end was very near, and like his contemporaries, he was mistaken. Having established to their own satisfaction the validity of this theory, all these scholars then hasten to point out that it really isn't very important anyway. The value of Jesus, they insist, does not rest upon a belief that he was endowed with infallible knowledge of future events. The fact that he was in error in expecting the imminent end of history does not in any way detract from his teaching on the nature of the Kingdom and its importance for man. The trend toward acceptance of this theory is so strong that some scholars now speak of it as an axiom of New Testament study.

But many others are not convinced, certain that there is a more coherent theory that fits the Synoptic picture of Jesus. According to this view, the extreme apocalyptic passages attributed to Jesus cannot be accepted as genuine. They do not fit in with the teaching of Jesus as a whole and they directly contradict Jesus' own warning about looking for signs of the end. These " warning " passages have about them a ring of authenticity, whereas the apocalyptic passages appear suddenly and introduce a jarring, discordant note into the message of Jesus. Moreover, these apocalyptic passages are quite easily accounted for.

In the first place, it is quite likely that many of the sayings of Jesus were misunderstood by his contemporaries because they were obsessed by apocalyptic speculation. Fully aware of the folly of nationalistic aspirations, Jesus predicted the destruction of the Temple in the event of military rebellion. It is easy to see how such predictions might be misread by those who were eagerly searching everywhere for signs of the end. There is ample evidence of this kind of misunderstanding throughout the Synoptics. In three successive chapters (chs. 8; 9; 10), Mark records how Jesus tried to teach his disciples the true nature of the kingly rule of God and of his own Messianic ministry. But in each case they simply could not comprehend what he was trying to say. They were too busy arguing among themselves about places of honor in the coming Kingdom. If his closest disciples misunderstood him in this way, it is not difficult to see how later writers could make the same mistake.

In the second place, it is relatively easy to account for the interpolation of apocalyptic passages in an age when the atmosphere was charged with expectancy, but it is impossible to account for Jesus' warnings against apocalyptic speculation unless the warnings came from Jesus himself. No one would think of placing such passages on his lips, for they were too much out of tune with the times. From the beginning of the nineteenth century, in fact, it has become increasingly evident to New Testament interpreters that most of the " Synoptic apocalypse " cannot be attributed to Jesus. The major portion of this material does not bear the stamp of Jesus at all, but sounds more like Enoch, Esdras, and numerous other apocalyptic writings of this period. The genuine intention of Jesus is found in those sayings counseling watchfulness. No man knows the day or the hour, not even the Son.

Jesus definitely believed that God would end history and bring his kingly rule to a glorious consummation. But he did not try to predict when the end would come. On the contrary, he denied having any special knowledge of such future events, counseling his followers to live in faithful and expectant watchfulness. In emphasizing the religious aspects of God's rule, he was often misunderstood by those whose minds were swept up in a consuming obsession with apocalypticism. Later writers interpolated current apocalyptic hopes, thus contradicting the genuine warnings of Jesus against this very thing, and it may well be that many modern New Testament scholars are making the same mistake, reading far too much apocalyptic speculation into the genuine message of Jesus.

C. THE SIGNIFICANCE OF ESCHATOLOGY

We have said that Jesus shared the general eschatological hopes of his people, but rejected apocalyptic predictions. He believed that God who is the sovereign Creator would in his own good time destroy the world, which man had defaced, and bring about a better order of things. He has now partially established his kingly rule and he will bring this to a glorious consummation at some future time by his own direct action. Meanwhile, it is imperative for men to accept the rule of God and live in holy obedience, leaving the end of all things in the hands of the Father.

This general eschatological teaching of Jesus emphasizes the sovereignty of God and gives a profound stimulus to the religious and ethical life of man. In this respect it is extremely significant, and no one can hope to understand the life and teaching of Jesus who disregards this eschatological framework. The loving Father who promises reconciliation to sinful men is the sovereign King of the universe whose glorious rule in all of its fullness is yet to come.

Emphasis upon the importance of eschatology in the teaching of Jesus should always be accompanied by a word of warning, however. Many men in every age have been so fascinated by speculation over the end of history that they miss the main point. The important thing is not history's end but present obedience to the kingly rule of God. It would be a tragedy to lose this pearl of great price in a maze of apocalyptic disputation.

There is a famous old story of a blind man who lived at the top of a mountain. Using his cane, he always made his way safely up the path when he returned home from a trip to the village. But one day he almost lost his life when he dropped his cane and leaned over the edge of the path in a vain attempt to retrieve it. His life was saved when he had presence of mind enough to stand up and lean back against the mountain, securely feeling his way along to his home on the summit. It would be a tragedy to lose our lives vainly feeling around for the answers to apocalyptic speculation when all we have to do to find our way home is to lean back securely on the mountain of God's forgiving love. Eschatology is important, but it is only one part of the riches of Christ's teaching. Acceptance *now* of the kingly rule of God is still the one thing needful.

13

Man and Reconciliation

A BRILLIANT young minister was once invited to deliver a sermon at the weekly worship service in the local state mental hospital. Unfortunately, he used an old sermon into which he had packed many long words and a good deal of meaningless generalization. Suddenly one of the patients stood up and said: " That's all very pretty, Reverend. But just what did you have in mind? " Since the young man didn't really have anything specific in mind, he soon pronounced the benediction and escaped in order to avoid further embarrassing questions.

One of the eternally appealing qualities of the teaching of Jesus is the way in which it avoids generalizations and deals with the specific needs of men. Jesus knew exactly what he had in mind for men to do and he made it explicitly clear. The bulk of his teaching, in fact, deals in a very specific way with the nature of man's response to the kingly rule of God and the nature of the new life that accompanies this response. The kingdom of God is his central theme, but he develops this theme principally in the direction of man's specific needs. In fact he spends so much time talking about man's ethical life under the rule of God that many people think of him primarily as a great ethical teacher. There is also a very common misunderstanding of the Christian religion among many modern followers of Jesus who think that being a Christian simply means living up to the ethical rules set forth by

Jesus. One of the great needs of modern Christianity is the correction of this grievous misapprehension.

Since Jesus had so much to say on this subject, it is helpful for purposes of study to break his teaching down into two basic premises and two basic experiences. Those who understand the premises and enter into the experiences will discover that they have " entered the Kingdom." The basic premises are: The purpose of man's life is to accept and live under the kingly rule of God; man has failed to fulfill this purpose. The basic experiences by which man overcomes this failure and fulfills the purpose of his life are: reconciliation; the new life.

A. The Purpose of Life

We have already emphasized the basic premise that motivated every aspect of Jesus' life and ministry. He was committed to the certainty that the purpose of man's life is to accept and live under the kingly rule of God. Gaining the Kingdom is the most important thing in life. It is worth the sacrifice of a hand, an eye, all of one's possessions, or anything else that stands in the way. It is the supreme good in life, the pearl of great price, the treasure hidden in a field, the one thing needful. When men seek first the Kingdom, then other things essential for life will be provided. The ultimate meaning of human life is thus found in the reign or Kingdom of God.

Until a man turns to God and accepts his rule, life is filled with frustration, anxiety, and despair. One of the strangest phenomena of modern times is man's obsessive search for peace of mind and happiness, for some purpose for living. Tragically, most of us are looking in the wrong places. Some are looking in the world outside, in people, activities, places, and things. Others are looking in isolation, fleeing from the world and living in cloistered poverty and humiliation. But all these seekers are doomed to failure, for they are looking in the wrong direction, and as a great German mystic said: " The longer they look, the less they find what they are looking for. They go along like someone who has missed his road; the farther they go, the more they go astray." Man's only peace is in God. There is a homing instinct within us, like the homing instinct of the birds, that leaves us restless and afraid until we turn to God. In every contact with persons, Jesus was intent upon helping them discover and fulfill this purpose for their creation.

B. Man's Predicament

With unerring insight, Jesus understood the nature of man's predicament. Man has failed to fulfill the purpose for his life. Instead of living under the rule of God, man is ruled by selfishness, pride, greed, insincerity, hatred, and lust. Instead of loving God, he loves himself and mammon. In short, man is a sinner, separated from God.

It must be emphasized clearly at this point that modern man's easygoing attitude toward sin is in direct opposition to the attitude of the Bible. Many persons do not like to discuss the matter and are quite offended if anyone suggests that they are " sinners." But the Biblical writers are realistic about the nature and universality of sin. They know, for example, that there are different levels of responsibility for our thoughts and actions. There is what might be called a descriptive definition: Sin is any action by a man that is contrary to his own judgment of what is right and wrong. The book of James puts it succinctly: " Whoever knows what is right to do and fails to do it, for him it is sin " (James 4:17). But obviously a man's own judgment does not constitute the ultimate norm of what is right and wrong. Therefore it is also necessary to hold to a more normative definition: Sin is disobedience to the will of God. This conception of sin runs through the entire Bible, starting in the Garden of Eden (Genesis) and ending with the final destruction of the world that results in the coming of the New Jerusalem (Revelation). In both these senses, the Bible insists on the universality of sin. Every man has failed to live up to his own moral judgment, and every man has disobeyed God. This Biblical doctrine is summed up by Paul: " All have sinned and fall short of the glory of God " (Rom. 3:23).

This is not the place to enter into a detailed discussion of the nature and prevalence of sin. It should be pointed out, however, that one of the major contributions of the modern neo-orthodox theologians has been their emphasis on the tragic reality and universality of sin. In this respect they are in complete accord with the thought of Jesus, who knew that all men are sinners and are separated from God because of sin. He spoke of the " adulterous and sinful generation " and of the " faithless and perverse generation." He told a moving parable of a diligent servant, ending with the troubling words, " And you also, when you have done all that is commanded you, say, ' We are unworthy servants ' " (Luke 17:10). He said that " no one is good but God alone " (Mark 10:18). He used many parables involving the experience of being lost or separated from the right place or the right way (cf. Luke, ch. 15). In the model prayer he taught men to pray, " Forgive us." He called upon men to repent and exhorted them to change their way of living, telling them that he had come to seek and to save the lost. Since Jesus is more interested in prescribing a cure than in diagnosing man's illness, he does not elaborate on the subject of sin. But it is perfectly obvious in every facet of his teaching that he is all too aware of the universal sinfulness of man and of the tragic separation from God that results.

The purpose of man's life is thus to accept and live under the rule of God. But man has failed to fulfill this purpose because of sin. Man is separated from God, going down the wrong road, and what is worse, the more he relies upon his own strength to overcome his sin, the more he sins! This is the " hopeless " predicament of man.

C. RECONCILIATION

Jesus knew that man's condition is far from hopeless. By relying on his own strength and resources to overcome sin, man has simply placed his hope in the wrong place. His true hope is grounded in the goodness of God. Jesus came preaching the gospel, the good news that God has provided a way for man to overcome his tragic predicament. No wonder the crowds listened to him with incredible gladness!

Man's basic need, according to Jesus, is to overcome the estrangement from God caused by his sin. This is accomplished through the basic experience of reconciliation or new birth. In this experience, man overcomes the power of sin and enters into a new relationship with God. He turns away from his old life of sin and enters into a new life of holy and joyful obedience to the will of God. He is like a man who has finally found his way home after wandering hopelessly lost in the abyss of sin and despair. Reconciliation is the primary experience of the Christian religion, for by it a man takes upon himself the yoke of the Kingdom. Modern Christianity is weak wherever we have watered down the interpretation and presentation of reconciliation. There are countless people who have grown up in the church who haven't the slightest comprehension of the meaning of this new birth, but any careful reading of the New Testament makes it clear that this is what the Christian religion is all about.

The report of Jesus' first sermon in Mark is one of the most important passages in the Bible, for it reveals the way in which a man becomes reconciled to God. " Now after John was arrested, Jesus came into Galilee, preaching the gospel of God, and saying, ' The time is fulfilled, and the kingdom of God is at hand; repent, and believe in the gospel.' " (Mark 1:14-15.) Thus Jesus announces that the rule of God is at hand, setting the central theme of his ministry amid an atmosphere of great urgency. " The time is fulfilled " means that the time foreseen by the prophets, the time set by God, has arrived. The fact that the Kingdom is " at hand " means that it has " begun to arrive." Then, after setting his theme, Jesus tells men what they must do to receive the Kingdom. This specific instruction falls into two parts: repentance and faith

("Repent, and believe the gospel"). Here we have in Jesus' own words the meaning of reconciliation.

Repentance is a "turning away" from sin toward God. It involves the awareness of sin as a present reality and a deep sorrow at the thought of its reign in our lives. When we feel sorrow at the ways in which misused freedom, old habits, and physical desire have led us away from God, we are beginning to understand the meaning of repentance. We may begin by feeling deep regret over specific things that we have done or left undone, but we soon realize that it is not just a few specific mistakes that separate us from God. Our whole condition needs forgiveness! Thus the burdened heart seeks God in deep contrition.

We are, then, much like the younger brother of the great Quaker mystic Rufus Jones, who reports that when quite small his younger brother carelessly got his hand caught in the blades of a mowing machine. Two fingers were cut off, and the night after the accident the small boy kept the whole family awake by crying out again and again: "I wish I hadn't done it! Oh, I wish I hadn't done it!" True repentance is the act in which a man looks at his true nature, sees everything that he has done to separate himself from God, and then cries out with the same pain and anguish, "I wish I hadn't done it!"

Jesus often repeated this call to repentance with which he opened his public ministry. He told men that he had come to call "sinners to repentance" (Luke 5:32). He spoke of the Galileans whom Pilate had killed and of those who died when the tower of Siloam fell. Then he said, "Unless you repent you will all likewise perish" (Luke 13:1-5). He later "began to upbraid the cities where most of his mighty works had been done, because they did not repent" (Matt. 11:20). When he sent the disciples out, he instructed them to preach "that men should repent" (Mark 6:12). And in dealing with distraught individuals such as Zacchaeus and Mary Magdalene, he first helped them feel the need for repentance. Jesus made it clear that the transaction of reconciliation between man and God begins with the deep contrition of repentance.

But repentance alone is not enough. If a man feels the weight of his sin without feeling hope, then he will ultimately despair. We need to know that we are accepted, loved, and forgiven in spite of our condition. We are then like the small boy in the orphanage who was visited by wealthy prospective parents. They had promised him toys, clothes, a room of his own, and many other fine things if he came to live with them. He replied, " If that is all you can give me, I would rather stay here with the other kids." " But why? " they demanded. " What on earth do you want? " He replied with deep feeling, " I want someone to love me! " This is exactly the way we feel when we see ourselves as we really are.

The good news that Jesus preached is that we do have someone to love us, that God in his goodness does accept, love, and forgive us when we turn to him in repentance. In his opening sermon, Jesus followed his call to repentance with a call for men to believe in this good news of God's forgiveness. " To believe," as Jesus used it, means to accept or welcome confidently and trustfully the forgiving love of God. It means to have faith in the good news of this divine forgiveness. When a truly repentant man opens his life fully to the forgiving love of God, reconciliation has been accomplished!

This is one of the reasons why Jesus emphasized so often the good news of God's love. The parables of the lost sheep, the lost coin, and the lost son all vividly illustrate the forgiving love of God and the joy in heaven when a sinner repents. Those who are in a condition to receive forgiveness, he said in another place, will receive forgiveness from a God who is eager to forgive. (Matt. 6:14.) Trust in this divine forgiving love is also implied in all that he said about faith. He told the disciples what they would be able to do if they had this faith (Luke 17:5-6), and he told those whom he had healed that their faith had made them well

(Mark 5:34). He said that the Kingdom belonged to those who had the expectant trust of children (Mark 10:13-16). Thus, for Jesus, man's hope for reconciliation lies in the unmerited, unexpected, oversurplus of forgiving love in God, what later Christians called "the grace of God."

This is why so many have described their experience of reconciliation with God as a "holy surprise." Driven to despair by the awareness of sin's hold on their lives, they know they deserve only punishment and death. But wonder of wonders and miracle of miracles — God reaches down and accepts them in forgiving love! No wonder they strain after analogies to describe their joy. They speak of a new light, of a peace that passes all understanding, of a joy unspeakable, of unsearchable riches, and of a new creation. They speak of lights going on, of bells ringing, of trumpets blowing. This is how a man feels when he has been reconciled to God through repentance and faith in the grace of God.

We have called this basic experience of the Christian religion *reconciliation* because it is fundamentally an overcoming of separation or estrangement from God. It is a many-sided experience, however, and it is not surprising that men approaching it in different ways have called it by different names. As a result of the conversation between Jesus and Nicodemus (John, ch. 3), it is often called *the new birth*. Just as a man is born once into the physical world, so he must be born again into a new spiritual world where he is reconciled to God. Following Paul, Martin Luther called the experience *justification,* making it the cornerstone of the Protestant Reformation. This simply means that through the grace of God a repentant man is suddenly recognized, "reckoned," as righteous. *Regeneration* is another New Testament word for the new birth. Other familiar terms used are *salvation* (being saved from sin to God), *redemption* (being set free from the bonds of sin), and *conversion* (turning away from sin to God). Many modern Christians are thoroughly confused by this array of terms, thinking that they refer to very different experiences. It must be emphasized, therefore, that all are simply different ways of explaining or describing the one basic experience of reconciliation. It should be noted, further, that this experience is the opposite of salvation by "works." Reconciliation with God cannot be purchased with any amount of good works or religious chores. It is not something we earn, but something we accept from a loving God in repentance and faith.

A good question bound to cause heated debate among any group of Christians is the question of how reconciliation comes — suddenly or gradually. For a long time, a conversion would scarcely be regarded as authentic unless it was sudden, accompanied by dramatic and sometimes violent manifestations, and witnessed by the faithful. This was the standard pattern, and deviations from the norm were definitely frowned upon. Now the standard pattern is the "gradual Christian," a very different thing. This person, we are told, born into a Christian home and gifted with a happy disposition, experiences reconciliation like "the unfolding of a flower." He does not need a sudden and violent turning toward God because he has been moving in that direction from the beginning. It cannot be doubted that there are genuine conversions of this gradual type, but the tragedy is that we use this phenomenon to cover up the fact that most young "Christians" today have had no experience at all! We are often assured that they are "unfolding like a flower," but the truth is, the bloom never appears.

Jesus did not waste time speculating about the ways in which this basic experience comes. He told Nicodemus it was like the wind — we do not know whence it comes or where it goes. It should not surprise us at all that such a deep transforming experience comes to people in different ways. But whether it comes gradually or suddenly, it should leave us with a feeling of holy surprise, unspeakable joy, contagious enthusiasm, and a consuming love for God and our fellows. If it has not done this to us, then we have probably not been reconciled at all!

In a very real way, the Christian religion revolves around this basic experience. When we say that we have been " saved through Christ," we simply mean that his life, death, and resurrection have revealed the way of reconciliation and made it possible for us now to live under the reign of God. When we emphasize the place of the cross in Christianity we do so because this event brings us to repentance and faith. On the cross we are involved in an experience of sin at its worst and love at its best to such a degree that we find ourselves " at one " with God (atonement). The sacrament of Baptism is an outward act symbolizing the cleansing from past sin (repentance) and acceptance of forgiveness from God (faith). Holy Communion is a renewing of reconciliation through remembrance of the atoning death of Christ. A careful reading of the Communion ritual reveals how repentance and divine grace are the recurring themes of worship. Thus the Christian religion is one that begins and continues for an individual when he is reconciled to the loving God through repentance and faith.

The modern Christian church desperately needs a new emphasis and interpretation of this basic experience. Countless church members think of Christian commitment in terms of obedience to rules or laws laid down by Christ and the church. Countless others have been brought into the church in " membership drives," never receiving any true insight into the nature of Christian experience. There are persons attending church every Sunday without feeling any surprise, joy, or enthusiasm at all. The old-time religion often overemotionalized the experience of reconciliation, whereas the new-time religion has all too often ignored it completely. But any study of the life and teaching of Jesus will reveal its continuing centrality for Christian faith. There is need for reinterpretation in terms of modern man's environment, but the basic experience remains the same. It is one of the unique features of Christianity, and apart from it the ethical teaching of Jesus is impossible and incomprehensible.

D. The New Life

The second basic Christian experience is a new life of holy obedience to the will of God. Reconciliation is a transforming experience that leads a man into a new kind of life. He is no longer the same person, becoming what Paul calls "a new creature," what Paul Tillich calls "a new being." This does not mean that he suddenly becomes perfect, but it does mean that he has a new motive for his actions and a new orientation for his thinking. He begins to live a life of love, not because he feels he must obey certain rules, but because he wants to. This new life growing out of reconciliation is so important that Jesus spent a good deal of time talking about it, describing in great detail the ways in which a person lives when he wants to obey the will of God. To this subject we now turn, remembering that this new life always grows out of the new birth — that experience of reconciliation made possible by the amazing grace of God.

14

Man and the New Life

ONE of the most common criticisms of the Christian church is that "Christians are no different from everyone else." In several years of ministering to a university community I have found this one of the most frequent complaints on the part of the younger generation. Sometimes the charge is made in a mood of bitterness or ridicule, but more often in wistful disappointment. Even those outside the church know that Christians are supposed somehow to be different from others, but many church members and some ministers appear totally unaware of this fact. Some even go out of their way to try to prove that they are just like everyone else in order to avoid embarrassing anyone who might be disturbed by his own Christian nonconformity.

Jesus made it perfectly clear that a new life, a different life, results from a man's new relationship to God when he enters the Kingdom. A reconciled man simply is not the same man he has been. Nor is it simply a matter of changing outward acts and words. He is transformed within, so that he literally becomes a "new person" living a new kind of life. Jesus, in fact, said that you can recognize those who are under the reign of God by the way they are living. "You will know them by their fruits." (Matt. 7:15-20.) He said that such persons are the salt of the earth, the light of the world. (Matt. 5:13-16.) Just as the purpose of salt is to give taste and the purpose of light is to give light, so the purpose of a reconciled man is to give flavor and light through his living. Anyone who claims to have found God in this new way but does not live this new life is as worthless as tasteless salt or a light under a bushel! In the story of the returning evil spirit he emphasized that it is not enough to sweep out the evil and to put our house in order. We must replace the evil with a positive life of obedience; otherwise, our last state becomes worse than the first. (Matt. 12:43-45.) Jesus made it unmistakably clear that a man's life is no longer the same when he has taken upon himself the yoke of the Kingdom. The new birth inevitably leads to a new life.

So important is this new life that Jesus spent most of his time talking about it. The bulk of his teaching is concerned with the description of this new kind of life, what it is, how it is motivated, where it leads. Since those reconciled to God want to live in this new way, Jesus provided them with a detailed blueprint of the new life in the Kingdom.

A. The Nature of the New Life

It must be emphasized at the beginning that the teaching of Jesus on this subject does not constitute a new " law." It is true that Jesus often quoted Jewish law and told his followers that he had come to fulfill it, but he opposed legalistic casuistry and hypocrisy in no uncertain terms, and he made it plain that mere obedience to the law was not enough. He said he had come to bring something new, a new wine that could not be stored in the old wineskins, a new patch that could not be used on old garments. His teaching simply could not be contained within the confines of legalism.

The tragedy is that the tendency has always been to turn the teaching of Jesus into a new law. It is surprising to discover how many people think of the Sermon on the Mount as a set of rules or laws laid down by Christ for his followers. By an act of resolution and strong will, a person makes an effort to live up to the law as laid down by Jesus. The Christian's primary duty thus becomes obedience to the law, and Christ becomes another Moses.

It is also a serious mistake to think of the teaching of Jesus as a system of ethics. Many great teachers have attempted to describe the ideal human character in terms of moral duty and behavior. Beginning with certain axioms, they build a system of complex principles and moral laws universally valid and rationally consistent. There have been many attempts to cast the ethical teaching of Jesus into just this kind of systematic ethical mold, but all such attempts are doomed to failure because they are based on false premises. The ethical teaching of Jesus simply will not pack down into neat compartments, and his personality defies every attempt to make him over into another Socrates or Immanuel Kant.

The ethical teaching of Jesus is absolutely unique in that it begins, not with moral laws or ethical principles, but with a complete transformation of character. He does not waste time with legalistic casuistry or rational arguments, knowing that the inner motivation of the person is the factor that ultimately determines moral conduct. A man does not obey because he "ought to" (moral law) or because it is more "reasonable" (philosophical ethics). He obeys because he has become a new being, a new person who *wants to* live the kind of life intended by God. Jesus, therefore, simply describes the new life, painting a picture for those who wish to know what it is like. He assumes that the lives of those who have been reconciled to God will bring forth this fruit as inevitably as a healthy tree sends forth its fruit in due season.

This is why joy has always been so prominent in the Christian faith. The little girl who said that she was not going back to a certain church "because nobody ever smiles there" had found a pretty good reason for not returning. Life for the Christian does not consist in grim obedience to oppressive external laws and principles. It consists rather in joyful obedience to the will of a

loving Father whose nature and presence have been discovered
through a new birth into a new kind of life. Many of the individual sayings of Jesus are not unique, but the basis of his ethical
teaching is wholly unique, for it is inseparably related to the
reconciling grace of God that makes all things new.

B. DESCRIPTION OF THE NEW LIFE

The new life in its simplest form is a life of conformity to the
will of God. In the Lord's Prayer, Jesus taught men to say, " Thy
kingdom come, thy will be done," thus giving in the second
phrase a definition of the first. He warned against the danger of
hypocrisy for those who claim to follow him: " Not every one
who says to me, ' Lord, Lord,' shall enter the kingdom of heaven,
but he who does the will of my Father who is in heaven " (Matt.
7:21-23). In Gethsemane, his own life reached its highest moment
when he prayed, " Not my will, but thine, be done." This is the
dominant prayer of the Christian, for when we enter the Kingdom of God we are eager to be found doing his will in all
things.

But it is not always easy to know just what the will of God may
be in a given situation. It is certainly easy to talk about doing
God's will. All kinds of bigots and fanatics have done this with
great conviction. The leaders of the ill-fated Children's Crusade
in the Middle Ages, the churchmen who burned Joan of Arc, the
witch burners of New England, many racial bigots of the twentieth century, all have claimed to be following the will of God.
In fact, those who crucified Jesus thought they were following the
divine will. It is not enough, therefore, to be told that the new
life is a life of obedience to the will of God. We must know more
specifically how we may determine his will.

Jesus therefore made his teaching more specific by saying that
the will of God is for man " to love." He made this clear in one
of the more familiar passages in the Gospels when he was asked
about the great commandment. It was not uncommon for the

rabbis to seek to summarize the law, and during the last week of Jesus' life, someone came to him seeking his answer to this problem. Jesus combined laws from Deuteronomy and Leviticus in his reply: " The first is, ' Hear, O Israel: The Lord our God, the Lord is one; and you shall love the Lord your God with all your heart, and with all your soul, and with all your mind, and with all your strength.' The second is this, ' You shall love your neighbor as yourself.' There is no other commandment greater than these " (Mark 12:29-31). Jesus did not define what he meant by " first," nor did he discuss the relation between the first and the second. He simply points out that love for God and neighbor summarizes the ethical duty of man.

It is impossible to appreciate the full importance of this passage without enlarging on the ordinary definition of the word " love." In English, this one word conveys many different meanings, but in the Greek there are many words for love. *Erōs* means erotic or physical love, *philia* means friendship or brotherly love. But Jesus did not use either of these words. He spoke of *agapē,* a creative, unselfish, universal love. This is a much deeper and more creative kind of love than that usually associated with our English word. The life of Jesus is the supreme example of *agapē* toward God and man.

The new life is a life in which the meaning of this kind of love is increasingly discovered and expressed. In every specific situation, those who are living under the reign of God are trying to apply *agapē* in increasingly meaningful ways. At the same time, this love leads them into a particular kind of relationship with one another, a mutual life-sharing at the deepest levels. When our three-year-old absolutely refused to stop sucking her thumb, even though the dentist said she was distorting the shape of her mouth, I said to her one day, " Debbie, sweetheart, I don't understand why a big girl like you has to suck her thumb all the time." Instantly she flashed back, " Well, you be Debbie and I'll be Daddy, and then you'll understand." This is the kind of empathic life-sharing that takes place when *agapē* is expressed toward others. We "become" the other person long enough to feel his needs and frustration and then we become ourselves again to minister with compassion learned from Christ. The Christian's love for God and neighbor is of this creative, universal kind, and the New Testament makes it clear that this is the kind of love God expresses for us. In fact, "God is *agapē*" (I John 4:8).

In the new life, therefore, obedience to the will of God simply means loving God and others in this creative way. Unfortunately, however, it is not always easy to know how to love. What actions and attitudes in our daily lives are true expressions of *agapē*? In specific situations in daily life we are often left with two alternatives, neither of which is the clear expression of love. What about defense of country in time of war, capital punishment of criminals, and mercy killing for persons in unbearable pain when death is inevitable? These and countless other questions arise when we honestly try to apply love. How can we know the best way to live in love?

Jesus answered this question by describing in great detail the specific ways in which *agapē* for God and man works itself out in daily life. Some persons look upon his many teachings on this subject as laws of humility, sincerity, and so on. But Jesus was simply spelling out in detail what it means to obey the will of God and live in *agapē*. The chart on the opposite page illustrates how he describes the new life in several ways, saying the same thing in each case, but making his description increasingly more specific and detailed. Thus obedience to the will of God means love for God and others. Love for God and others leads to certain specific acts and attitudes such as those suggested below. We may thus describe the new life in any one of three ways: (1) Obedience to the will of God, (2) Love (*agapē*) for God and others, (3) The practice of specific virtues, such as humility, sincerity, service to others, forgiveness, courage, and detachment from things.

It is not necessary to enter into a detailed interpretation of the

ETHICS OF JESUS
(The New Life)

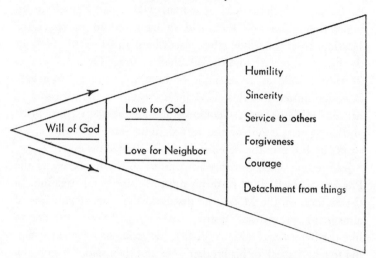

Will of God

Love for God

Love for Neighbor

Humility

Sincerity

Service to others

Forgiveness

Courage

Detachment from things

specific acts and attitudes discussed by Jesus because in each case his main intention is quite clear. It is worth noting, however, how he gave increasing attention to this subject, apparently believing that it was extremely important to paint the picture of the new life as clearly as possible.

The attitude of *humility* was a matter of great concern to Jesus. He spent a good deal of time talking about it and warning men of the dangers of pride. The spiritual conceit of the Pharisees may partially account for this unusual concern, but Jesus makes it plain that pride in any form is particularly dangerous because it means that we are trusting in ourselves rather than in God. It also means that we are expressing superiority rather than compassion for others. Pride, therefore, is a flagrant denial of love for both God and neighbor! In one striking parable, Jesus contrasted the proud Pharisee and the humble publican, concluding, " I tell you, this man went down to his house justified rather than the other; for every one who exalts himself will be humbled, but he who humbles himself will be exalted" (Luke 18:9-14). He used exactly the same words at the conclusion to the parable of the banquet in which he told of a man who seated himself in an honored position and then had to be asked to move (Luke 14:7-14). In at least four other places he says, "Behold, many of the first shall be last, and the last shall be first." On one occasion he used a child as an example of humility, saying, "Whoever humbles himself like this child, he is greatest in the kingdom of heaven" (Matt. 18:4). Genuine humility, freedom from pride and arrogance, is one of the very definite ways in which *agapē* works itself out in the new life of the reconciled believer.

Jesus emphasized *sincerity* in contrast to the hypocrisy of the Pharisees, which called forth his most scathing condemnation. In the Sermon on the Mount, he discussed the current practices of almsgiving, prayer, and fasting, concluding, "You must not be like the hypocrites" (Matt. 6:1-18). He spoke of a person straining to take a speck of his brother's eye and then said, "You hypocrite, first take the log out of your own eye, and then you will see clearly to take the speck out of your brother's eye" (Matt. 7:1-5). Later, he condemned many practices of the Pharisees, beginning each saying with the warning, "Woe to you, scribes and Pharisees, hypocrites!" He insisted on agreement between inner motive and outward act, knowing that any false appearance of virtue prevented the development of insights necessary for growth in the practice of love.

Compassion or active *service to others* is one of the most obvious expressions of *agapē*. How can we love others without showing ourselves eager to serve them in their need? Jesus emphasized the universality of this kind of love when he told the story of the good Samaritan, regarded by many as the greatest of his parables (Luke 10:37). Here is the expression of a love that does not stop to ask questions or make excuses, but moves instantly to meet human need. Every man we meet is a neighbor to be loved, no matter how many outward differences divide us. In the parable of the rich man and Lazarus, the rich man is in Hades because he had an opportunity to help the poor but did not (Luke 16:19-31). The parable of the Last Judgment places an even greater emphasis on acts of love and compassion, implying that a man's salvation depends upon the ways in which he has moved to meet the needs of others (Matt. 25:31-46). When we remember the compassion of Jesus during his ministry, and witness the continuing philanthropic interest of Christianity, it is not surprising to find some commentators speaking of this active good will toward others as the most characteristic Christian virtue.

Jesus insisted on unconditional *forgiveness* in contrast to the hatred and retaliation that break down man's relationship with God and others. He shocked his listeners by setting aside the old law of retaliation (" an eye for an eye, a tooth for a tooth "), demanding love and forgiveness even to the second mile (Matt. 5:38-42). He also set aside the old idea of love for friends and hatred for enemies: "I say to you, Love your enemies and pray for those who persecute you " (Matt. 5:43-48). The absolute stand taken by Jesus on this matter troubled Peter, who came to Jesus asking, "Lord, how often shall my brother sin against me and I forgive him? As many as seven times? " Jesus replied, "I do not say to you seven times, but seventy times seven " (Matt. 18:21-22). Following the Lord's Prayer, Jesus pointed out how forgiveness is related to man's love for God. "If you forgive men their trespasses, your heavenly Father also will forgive you; but if you do not forgive men their trespasses, neither will your Father forgive your trespasses." (Matt. 6:14-15.) This is not a bargain with God, but a simple truth based on the fact that those who do not forgive others are in no position to understand and receive the forgiveness of God. It should be pointed out that Jesus poignantly underlined every word he had spoken on this subject when he looked down from the cross and asked God's forgiveness for those who were killing him (Luke 23:34).

Jesus emphasized *courage* in his teaching, making it clear

from the beginning that it would not be easy to obey the will of God. To a vacillating follower he said, "No one who puts his hand to the plow and looks back is fit for the kingdom of God" (Luke 9:62). He asked his disciples if they were willing to drink the cup of suffering, to take up a cross, to renounce all that they had. In preparing them for the future he warned them of suffering to come and told them to count the cost before setting out. It would take courage to love God in all times and in all places. It would take even more courage to love others in a world that often looked upon love as weakness.

Finally, Jesus often spoke of the necessity of *detachment from material things* in the new life of obedience to the will of God. "No one," he said, "can serve two masters; for either he will hate the one and love the other, or he will be devoted to the one and despise the other. You cannot serve God and mammon." (Matt. 6:24.) He warned against storing up treasures on earth, for "where your treasure is, there will your heart be also" (Matt. 6:19-21). He told the parable of a rich fool who set aside material wealth for the future and then died before he could enjoy it (Luke 12:13-21). After meeting a rich young man who refused to follow him because of financial wealth, Jesus uttered a warning that has troubled the comfortable ever since: "Children, how hard it is to enter the kingdom of God! It is easier for a camel to go through the eye of a needle than for a rich man to enter the kingdom of God" (Mark 10:24-25). Those who are living under the reign of God, he said, should not be anxious about food and clothing but should "seek first his kingdom and his righteousness, and all these things shall be yours as well" (Matt. 6:25-33). Some persons interpret these passages as revolutionary doctrine, concluding that Jesus was against wealth on principle, but he never said that mammon was either good or evil in itself. The danger is that man will become so attached to his possessions that he is no longer attached to God, and so wrapped up in his own wealth that he becomes insensitive to the poverty of others. When a man loves his money he cannot love God and neighbor.

Even though Jesus spent most of his time talking about these specific aspects of the new life, it should be emphasized again that he was not laying down a new code of laws or ethical principles. He was simply describing the new life of joyful and holy obedience that grows out of the new birth. Through reconciliation a man finds God in an experience that leaves him with a consuming desire to live this new kind of life of creative love.

C. The Sermon on the Mount

In three chapters of Matthew (chs. 5 to 7) there appears a discourse of Jesus' that has had an incomparable influence on human history. The Sermon on the Mount, an epitome of the ethical teaching of Jesus, has influenced Christians and non-Christians alike. Tolstoy, Gandhi, and a host of others have recognized the unique value of this teaching, Gandhi once having said that the world's problems would be solved if men would live by the principles of this sermon.

Unfortunately, the Sermon on the Mount has been misunderstood by those who feel that it contains a complete summary of the teaching of Jesus. Others look upon it as an expression of the new Christian law or as a set of rules to be followed by those who call themselves Christians. On the contrary, the Sermon is simply a concise, artistic description of the new life of love (*agapē*). It presupposes both the reign of God as the supreme expression of God's purpose for man and reconciliation as the experience by which a man accepts that reign. Very little is said directly about either of these great themes. Jesus sets out, rather, to illustrate the ideal life of those who have been reconciled to God and are now living in obedience to his will. The Sermon on the Mount is in many ways the masterpiece of Jesus, but it must be viewed within the framework of the Kingdom and against the background of reconciliation.

A simple outline illustrates how the new life stands out as the dominant theme of the Sermon:

THE SERMON ON THE MOUNT

(Matt., chs. 5 to 7)
I. Characteristics of the New Life (ch. 5:3-16)
   A. Description (vs. 3-12)
   B. Influence (vs. 13-16)
II. Relation of the New Life to the Old Order
      (chs. 5:17 to 6:18)
   A. Summary (ch. 5:17-20)
   B. Morality (ch. 5:21-48)
   C. Piety (ch. 6:1-18)
III. Devotion to God in the New Life (ch. 6:19-34)
   A. Possessions (vs. 19-24)
   B. Anxiety (vs. 25-34)
IV. Various Counsels on the New Life (ch. 7:1-27)
   A. Sayings (vs. 1-12)
   B. Conclusion (vs. 13-27)

This Sermon brings out better than any other utterance of Jesus' the new basis that he gives to the practice of the good life. All other religious and philosophical ethics, as we have seen, are handed down in the form of laws or principles of conduct. Man's outward conduct is measured against these external standards. Jesus is unique in that he placed his emphasis first of all upon a fundamental inner change, a change of character. He did not apply new laws or principles to the same person, but began with a new person and illustrated how new outward conduct results from inner transformation. He spoke often about outward conduct, but always as a result of inner motivation or desire. Jesus did not offer a new system of ethics but a whole new approach to ethics. The fact that many of his followers interpret this teaching in terms of legalism does not detract from the uniqueness of his contribution to the moral life of man.

The uniqueness of this fundamental new approach to ethics explains why the Sermon on the Mount appears so radical, even impossible, at first, and then becomes so practical. G. K. Chesterton once remarked that the Sermon on the Mount " turns everything upside down, but later you discover that it turns everything right side up." This is true only because we have been living in a topsy-turvy world of our own making. When we experience a new birth and begin to live a new life, then we enter into a world of God's making where there is a peace and joy passing all human understanding.

15

Messiah and Son of God

J ESUS came preaching the good news that God's reign was at hand. This was the central theme of his message from the first sermon in Galilee to the last farewells in Judea. From the beginning, however, the message was intimately related to the person who brought the message, so much so that "Kingdom of God" and "Jesus Christ" have become synonymous terms in the minds of many believers. This is true to such an extent that those who enter the Kingdom take upon themselves his name, calling themselves Christians.

But who was he? In many ways he remains history's greatest enigma, revealing fully the nature of God but never fully revealing the nature of his own person. For several centuries the church debated about how to explain their conviction that he was both human and divine, finally retreating behind the term "mystery." Albert Schweitzer says Jesus comes as unknown to us as he came to those beside the lake, an ineffable mystery, and he remains unknown until we learn in our own experience who he is. The experience of some leads them to believe that he is the greatest teacher who ever lived. Others are certain he is God. Countless titles have been applied to him: Messiah, Son of God, Redeemer, Savior, Lord, Lamb of God, Word of God, Emmanuel, Prince of Peace, Light of the World, Good Shepherd, King of Kings. Each title is an attempt to describe some phase of his life or work, but taken separably or together, titles cannot capture the feelings of those who have known him. Every attempt to "explain" Jesus ultimately fails, yet such attempts are inevitable.

This present work is not a study of Christology. It is a contribution to Christology, however, for we cannot understand Jesus until we know what he said about himself. His own words should be the starting point for theological discussion of this subject on every level. The relevant material falls into three general categories: Jesus' words about himself as prophet, Messiah, and Son of God.

A. Prophet

It is quite plain from the records that the crowds at first took Jesus for a prophet. "A great prophet has arisen among us!" they reported in amazement. Jesus apparently accepted this designation, looking upon himself as one who followed in the tradition of the great prophets of the Old Testament. He often quoted their words and did not seem surprised when Peter reported that people thought he was Elijah, Jeremiah, or one of the prophets. When he was rejected at Nazareth, he pointed out that "no prophet is acceptable in his own country" (Luke 4:16-30). When told that Herod wanted to kill him, Jesus replied, "Nevertheless I must go on my way today and tomorrow and the day following; for it cannot be that a prophet should perish away from Jerusalem" (Luke 13:33).

Few persons would disagree with the conclusion that Jesus was a great prophet. Even Jewish scholars such as Rabbi Klausner and radical historians such as Guignebert agree. The question is, Was he more than a prophet? He certainly claimed more authority than was normal for a prophet, and his own followers soon applied titles to him that indicated that he was for them far more than a mere prophetic spokesman for God.

Charles Lamb was once in a group of men who were discussing what they would do if certain great men suddenly appeared in their midst. When the name of Jesus was mentioned, Lamb remarked that if other great men appeared, they would all rise but that if Jesus appeared, they would all kneel. Men in every age have felt this reverence, showing that among all who have known him is the feeling that he is far more than a prophet.

B. The Messiah

"Messiah," from the Hebrew for "anointed one," refers to the expected divinely appointed leader who would inaugurate the rule of God. The idea of the Messiah, reaching far back into the Old Testament period, followed many divergent lines of development. As we have seen, however, most of the contemporaries of Jesus thought of the Messiah as a worldly hero, a political and military leader in the pattern of King David. The one unifying idea in all speculation concerning the Messiah was that his coming was to be the signal for the opening of the new age of the reign of God.

It is quite obvious that Jesus knew himself to be the Messiah. The Messianic claim is implicit in the stories of the baptism and temptation. When the mentally ill recognized him as the Messiah and when Peter first confessed this conviction, Jesus did not disavow their claim. In the first sermon reported by Luke, he read a Messianic passage from Isaiah and then said, " Today this Scripture has been fulfilled in your hearing." The triumphal entry is clearly the enactment of a Messianic prophecy, and the death of Jesus is unintelligible apart from the Messianic claim. When the high priest asked him directly, " Are you the Christ? " he replied, " I am," thereby convicting himself. Jesus definitely looked upon himself as the long-expected Messiah, the person through whom God's rule was being realized.

The specific development of his Messianic ministry, however, was largely determined by the fact that he was not the kind of Messiah people expected. We have already seen how family, friends, and enemies all misunderstood him. In three successive chapters in Mark's Gospel (chs. 8;9;10), Jesus tried to instruct his disciples in the meaning of his Messiahship, but in each case they misinterpreted his intentions. The pathetic words of the two heartbroken disciples who walked the road to Emmaus sum up the expectations of all his followers: " We had hoped that he was the one to redeem Israel " (Luke 24:21). According to their last question to him in the Book of Acts they misunderstood to the very end: " Lord," they asked, " will you at this time restore the kingdom to Israel? " (Acts 1:6).

These misguided expectations explain why Jesus did not speak more openly and directly of his Messianic vocation. The so-called " Messianic secret " has been one of the serious problems of Gospel study from the very beginning. If Jesus was the Messiah, why didn't he say so? In the Synoptic Gospels he goes out of his way to try to keep it a secret, silencing the demoniacs, telling those whom he has healed to tell no one, even charging his disciples to be silent about it. When John the Baptist inquired about him he veiled his affirmative answer. In the Q document there is no direct declaration at all, in Mark only the one admission before the high priest. In view of this evidence, some interpreters have insisted that Jesus did not believe himself to be the Messiah.

It is much more reasonable, however, to assume that he felt the necessity of instructing his listeners concerning the meaning of the Messiahship before he could declare himself to be the Messiah. Otherwise they would instantly jump to the wrong conclusions and bring disaster upon themselves and upon him. He had to tell them what kind of Messiah to expect before he could tell them that he was that Messiah.

According to Mark's Gospel, he gradually unfolded his own Messianic claim as his followers grew in understanding. Mark records six definite stages in this unveiling of the Messianic secret: (1) to Jesus alone at his baptism (Mark 1:11); (2) to the mentally ill early in his ministry (chs. 1:24; 3:11); (3) to Peter at Caesarea Philippi (ch. 8:27-33); (4) to the disciples as a group (chs. 9:31 f.; 10:33 f.); (5) to the crowd during his triumphal entry (ch. 11:1-10); (6) to everyone present during his trial before the high priest when he admitted, "I am" (ch. 14:61-62). These definite stages are sometimes blurred in the other Gospels, but Mark has apparently recorded a definite strategic move on the part of Jesus. He revealed the fact of his Messianic vocation only as fast as he could impart its true meaning.

The Messianic title that Jesus chose for himself also indicates his definite but veiled Messianic claim. There are many such Messianic titles applied to Jesus by others, but only "Son of man" has his authority. The term occurs in the Synoptics some seventy times and always on the lips of Jesus. It is quite ambiguous, however, having previously been used in several different ways: (a) In the Old Testament generally it is used to refer to man. "What is man that thou art mindful of him, and the son of man that thou dost care for him?" (Ps. 8:4.) (b) In The Book of Daniel, it is used in a special sense as a name for the kingdom of the saints of the Most High (Dan. 7:13-14), in other words, the future Messianic community. (c) In the book of Enoch (an extremely popular apocalyptic writing composed in the century before Christ) the term is used to describe a pre-existent spiritual being who dwells in heaven and is about to appear on earth.

"Son of man" was a Messianic title, but one with many meanings. Since its usage was not yet definitely fixed in the minds of his hearers, Jesus could invest the term with new Messianic meaning and apply it to himself. The adoption of this title is a definite part of his plan to reveal himself in a new and unexpected Messianic role.

It should be noted, finally, that the most shocking and unacceptable aspect of his Messianic teaching was his conviction that the Messiah would suffer and die. The concept of the Suffering Servant that he adopted for himself had been one of the great contributions of Old Testament thought to the history of Israel. The people of Israel realized that they were "chosen" to serve the Lord through suffering. But no one had connected the idea of the Suffering Servant with that of the Messiah who was to be a conquering king! (Cf. Isa. 52:13 to 53:12.)

It is part of the startlingly original contribution of Jesus that he combined the idea of the Suffering Servant with that of the Messiah. The divine agent who would inaugurate the Kingdom would come as one who serves, not as one who rules. Suffering, pain, humiliation, and death would be a necessary part of his ministry to others. Every time the disciples gave any indication of recognizing his Messianic vocation, Jesus tried to tell them that this meant suffering and death. "The Son of man must suffer many things. . . . The Son of man also came not to be served but to serve, and to give his life as a ransom for many." (Mark 8:31; 10:45.) "I am among you as one who serves." (Luke 22:27.) "This is my blood of the covenant, which is poured out for many." (Mark 14:24.) This concept which Jesus adopted as the very essence of his Messianic vocation was the chief stumbling block to everyone who came out of the Jewish faith. It is at the same time one of the unique and creative contributions of Jesus, for it reveals the incredible truth that the highest purposes of God are fulfilled through suffering!

C. THE SON OF GOD

Jesus believed and taught that he was the Suffering Servant Messiah, but even this does not explain the extraordinary devotion to him as a person exhibited by countless of his followers in every age. In times of persecution they have been fed to the lions, hung on crosses, and burned alive. In other times they have been ridiculed and reviled, only to cling more closely to the one who has claimed their undefiled loyalty. Ignatius of Antioch, who lived in the second century, is typical. On the journey to Rome where he was to be fed to wild animals in the amphitheater, he wrote to his friends, "Come fire and iron, come rattling of wild beasts, cutting and mangling and wrenching of my bones, come hacking of my limbs, come crushing of my whole body, come cruel tortures of the devil to assail me! Only be it mine to attain to Jesus Christ." But persons were not committed to Jesus in this way simply because he was the Messiah. They had known him as the Messiah, but they had also known him as the Son of God.

In a certain sense all men are sons of God, and Jesus, insisting that God is a Father, supports this idea. The New Testament, however, makes it quite clear that Jesus is not *a* son of God, but *the* Son of God in a unique way. This raises the question, Did Jesus believe this and teach it about himself?

This is an extremely important question, for throughout this study we have interpreted the unique insight and power of Jesus in terms of his own filial consciousness of God. We have insisted that he knew himself to be the Son of God, constantly growing in awareness of God's presence and in obedience to his will. The divinity of Jesus is not only a matter of external authority " from above " but of filial consciousness and obedience from within.

Even at the age of twelve he spoke of " my Father's house." At the time of his baptism he heard the voice of God saying, " Thou art my beloved Son." Throughout his life he referred to God as " my Father," and on the last day of his life directly admitted that he was " the Christ, the Son of the Blessed " (Mark 14:61-62). The parable of the wicked tenants is especially meaningful in this connection, since it is a story intended to show how all of God's previous messengers to Israel had been slaves or servants, whereas Jesus is the one "beloved Son " of the Father (Mark 12:1-9).

One of the most important Christological verses in the New Testament also appears in the Synoptic Gospels on the lips of Jesus. It is the second part of the so-called " great thanksgiving " in Matthew: " All things have been delivered to me by my Father; and no one knows the Son except the Father, and no one knows the Father except the Son and any one to whom the Son chooses to reveal him " (Matt. 11:27). This direct sense of " unshared sonship" is unmatched even in the Gospel of John where this becomes a central theme. Jesus knew himself to be the Son of God, and this unique filial consciousness contributed a divine dimension to every word and act of his life. The author of John built his Gospel on this conviction, but it is just as obvious in the Synoptics, where Jesus is *the* Son of God.

But John, Paul, and all later Christians have had the greatest difficulty in explaining "how" he was the Son of God. How could any fully human person be at the same time fully divine? The fact of his complete humanity has been an established certainty among his followers from the beginning. There have been attempts to reject his full humanity, often by well-meaning Christians overzealous in their efforts to defend his divinity. These persons would do well to hearken to the words of Luther, "The beginning of all our theology is in the humanity of Jesus." On the other hand, there has been just as great an insistence on his full divinity. He is not just a great teacher, nor is he simply a man with godlike qualities. He is the Son of God, divine in nature, partaking of the very nature of God himself.

Many attempts to explain the true nature of Christ have ended in the realm of mystery. The Creed of Chalcedon, formulated in A.D. 451, was the fruition of generations of study and debate. But this creed merely stated the problem: Christ is truly human, Christ is truly divine, Christ is truly divine-human. Still, the Christian mind has been unwilling to rest with this kind of formulation and continues to seek words to describe the deeper meaning of the person of Christ.

Unfortunately, many modern Christians believe they solve the problem by stating flatly, "Jesus is God." Anyone who has known Christ will sympathize with what they are trying to say, but it must be pointed out that this statement is nowhere made by Jesus or by any writer in the New Testament. On the contrary, Jesus always went out of his way to emphasize his subordinate position to God. "Why do you call me good?" he said.

"No one is good but God alone." (Mark 10:18.) "Not I, but the Father," he often said, thus pointing away from himself. He prayed to God in agony, an act that becomes meaningless if he was God. Even in John's Gospel, which has probably the most exalted view of his divinity in the New Testament, it is quite clear that there is no intention to equate Jesus with God. He prayed to "the only true God" as the one who "didst send me" (John, ch. 17). This is the prayer, in fact, that contains the statement, "I and the Father are one," which is so often used by those who maintain that Jesus is God. If such persons would continue reading, they would discover Jesus praying that the disciples "may be one, even as we are one" (v. 11). Surely Jesus is not praying for a metaphysical unity that would mean that the disciples are God! On the contrary, our records make it clear that Jesus pointed away from himself to God. He was "the way" to God, he was "the door" to God. He did not say, "I am God."

It must be maintained just as strongly, however, that Jesus knew himself to be the Son of God, partaking fully of the divine nature. We have already seen the evidence in the Synoptics that every other New Testament writer would support. In some very real sense, Jesus was the fulfillment of God's eternal plan. God prepared for the coming of Jesus and called him to reveal the nature of the Kingdom to men. God calls every individual to fulfill a purpose in his creation, but the call that came to Jesus was utterly unique. Only Jesus was called to be Messiah and Son of God.

In faithful obedience, Jesus responded to this call, constantly growing in understanding of the will of God and in consciousness of the presence of God. Part of the wonder of his life is God's grace guiding him and empowering him. Part of the wonder is his own free choice of the way of obedience. His free response to God's call is, like the call itself, utterly unique. No one else has even approached the degree of obedience to the will of God that is evident in Jesus. He exhibited in his own life total and unconditional acceptance of the reign of God.

All our Gospel records give evidence of increasing growth in the relationship between Father and Son. With increasing commitment, he identified his purpose with the purpose of God. His will became "one" with the will of God. His consciousness became more and more a consciousness of the fullness of God. Thus the identity of will and purpose became so complete that when Jesus spoke or acted, the will of God was speaking and acting through him. This accounts for the statements of Jesus in which he subordinates himself to God as well as those in which he expresses his unique consciousness of being the one "beloved Son" of the Father.

Any attempt to interpret the person of Jesus that is true to his own teaching must emphasize both the grace of God and the free choice of Jesus: on the one hand, God's eternal plan, God's call, God's continuing guidance in love; on the other hand, Jesus' free response, his growing understanding, and his increasing obedience in love. If we start with one of these, we will speak of the way in which God became man. If we start with the other, we will try to show how a man became divine. There is truth in both directions, as we see in the tendency of the New Testament writers to say both of these things at once. John says that "the Word became flesh and dwelt among us, full of grace and truth" (John 1:14), thus beginning with God. Acts, on the other hand, beginning with the man Jesus, says "God has made him both Lord and Christ, this Jesus whom you crucified" (Acts 2:36).

From the very beginning, those who knew Jesus were convinced that in him they beheld the fullness of the one true God. There was no other way to explain his influence over them. Heywood Broun once wrote a memorable newspaper column describing a drunken artist who etched a portrait of Christ on the wall of his jail cell. From that time on, strange transformations began to occur in the lives of those who occupied that cell. They could not escape the creative influence of this person, Jesus the Christ. Countless others, feeling this same influence, have tried to describe it and interpret it. Hearkening back to the conviction of Jesus himself, they are certain that he is not just a great prophet or even Messiah. He is the true Son of God's love.

CONCLUSION

16

The Gospel of John

THE GOSPEL of John is in many ways the masterpiece of the Bible. It has many things in common with the Synoptic Gospels, but is definitely in a class of its own. The author was one of those rare figures in history who combine superb talent with deep religious insight. In this sense he was like Michelangelo, who painted the Sistine Chapel; Dante, who wrote the *Divine Comedy;* or Handel, who composed *The Messiah.* Each used his own particular talent to create a religious masterpiece of unsurpassed power and artistic beauty. The author of the Fourth Gospel used his religious, intellectual, and literary genius to create a book unmatched in the religious literature of the world. Those who begin to sound its depths will understand why it has always been the favorite Gospel of millions.

The portrait of Jesus painted by this writer is very different from that given in the Synoptics. As we have seen, they had certain peculiar characteristics and a definite family resemblance, but John has a purpose all his own: " Now Jesus did many other signs in the presence of the disciples, which are not written in this book; but these are written that you may believe that Jesus is the Christ, the Son of God, and that believing you may have life in his name " (John 20:30-31). This purpose is obvious in the atmosphere that the author creates from the opening line to the last, and it determines his style as well as his choice of material. Since this is a canonical Gospel, it is invaluable in the study of the life and teaching of Jesus, but it is a unique Gospel, demanding the most careful interpretation and evaluation.

A. CHARACTERISTICS OF THE GOSPEL

By the time John wrote, the salient features of the life and teaching of Jesus were matters of common knowledge. He did not intend, therefore, to record the career of Jesus but to interpret the meaning of that career. He wrote a spiritual or theological Gospel, knowing that his readers would already be familiar with the Synoptics. Taking a few events from the life of Jesus, he elaborated upon their meaning and related them to his central purpose, which was to show that Jesus is the Christ, the Son of God. Even the Synoptics reflect a certain amount of theological interpretation, but John has carried this to the extreme. His main interest is in the theological or spiritual meaning of the words and acts of Jesus.

It has been suggested that the two main sections of a modern newspaper roughly illustrate the contrast between the Synoptics and John. The front page of a newspaper features the top news stories of the day, recording the pertinent facts of time, place, and circumstance. The editorial page, on the other hand, takes a few incidents from the day's news and interprets their meaning, emphasizing their relevance and their relationship to other timely issues. Roughly speaking, the Synoptic Gospels give us the news story of Jesus, whereas John gives us the editorial page. He turns the healing of a blind man or a casual conversation into a whole chapter, reinterpreting the events in terms of his own experience and that of the religious community of his own time.

His uppermost concern throughout is to probe and express the innermost thoughts of Jesus himself. He wants to reveal the consciousness of Jesus to his readers, to record not the actual words of Jesus but his actual thoughts and intentions. In doing this, he has given the ideas a form characteristic of his own mode of thinking, just as Plato has recorded the thought of Socrates in a "Platonic" dialogue form. The Fourth Gospel presents the thought of Jesus in a Johannine form that is totally unlike the Synoptics. By this means we gain deeper insight into the mind of Jesus, as the author amplifies themes and ideas that are only hinted at in the Synoptics.

Until the nineteenth century the Gospel was almost universally accepted as the work of John Zebedee, one of the Twelve. It is now relatively certain that it is a late work, coming from the first decade of the second century. This conclusion, based on comparative studies of literary style and religious content, has tended to undermine the theory of Johannine authorship, although the author may have been a disciple of John Zebedee. Whoever he was, his keen intellect, his religious genius, and his dramatic style are reflected on every page of his work.

It is fairly obvious that the author was a Palestinian Jew, exhibiting close familiarity with the thought of Judaism and with the country of Palestine. His ideas are fundamentally Jewish in nature, based on the Old Testament conviction that the purpose of the eternal God is manifest in the events of history. Many interpreters have insisted that this Gospel is the most characteristically Jewish work in the New Testament. At the same time he is familiar with the thought of the Greeks, often relating philosophical ideas to the thought of Jesus. The discovery of the Dead Sea scrolls has also brought to light the author's unusually intimate knowledge of sectarian Judaism (the Essenes). In a very real sense his book is a synthesis of traditional Judaism, Hellenism, and sectarian Judaism.

This book is obviously a Gospel since its purpose is to announce the "good news." It is likely that the author knew the Synoptics well, for he followed the same general outline of the life of Jesus, supplementing and correcting where he thought it necessary. In some places he adopted phrases and ideas from the other Gospels and in other places he assumed that his readers already knew the facts of Jesus' life.

In spite of this dependence on others, however, John wrote in splendid isolation as far as style and content are concerned. He records the teaching of Jesus in an unmistakable Johannine style that omits the parables and short sayings of Jesus. These are replaced by long discourses on recurring themes, all cast in an allegorizing style in which every word is "loaded" with a double meaning. The ministry expands from one year to three in this Gospel, and most of it takes place in Jerusalem rather than in Galilee. There is no Messianic secret here, Jesus openly declaring his Messiahship from the beginning, with others recognizing him as Messiah. The cleansing of the Temple occurs right at the start of the ministry and the Last Supper on the day before Passover in a radical departure from the Synoptics. The baptism, the temptation, the transfiguration, and the agony in Gethsemane are all omitted. The raising of Lazarus is added, but there is no account of the institution of the Eucharist in the upper room. Quite apparent in the book is the author's desire to refute the claims of synagogue Judaism and the sect of John the Baptist, neither of which was a serious threat when the Synoptics were written.

He sets the theme of his Gospel in a matchless prologue in which Jesus is presented as the incarnate Word of God, then moves into the story of the public ministry, which he builds around a framework of seven miracle stories and a series of discourses and dialogues. The raising of Lazarus, for example, is the perfect vehicle for presenting Christ as one who brings new life to all those who are dead spiritually. It is extremely difficult, if not impossible, to determine where history ends and allegory begins. Doubly meaningful also are the upper room discourses of Jesus, which this Gospel records at length. The book ends with the most dramatic and vivid Passion narrative in any of our records, followed by the resurrection, God's final revelation through the Word made flesh. Any careful reading of this Gospel reveals a startling simplicity coupled with a theological pro-

fundity, which soon carry the reader out beyond his depth. One
thing is certain: the author's style and ideas are distinctively his
own, in many ways bringing us closer to Jesus than any other
book in the New Testament.

B. The Son of God

The author of this Gospel offers a rich and suggestive interpretation of the teaching of Jesus. He develops themes that are only
briefly suggested in the Synoptics and he tries to show how the
teaching of Jesus grew out of the inner filial consciousness that
he felt in his relationship with God. Two themes stand out as
the main burden of the author's thought: "Jesus as the Son of
God" and "eternal life." John states his own definite reasons for
writing at the end of the book (ch. 21 is an appendix): "Now
Jesus did many other signs in the presence of the disciples, which
are not written in this book; but these are written that you may
believe that Jesus is the Christ, the Son of God, and that believing
you may have [eternal] life in his name" (ch. 20:30-31). By his
own admission, he states that his intention is to write about Jesus
as the Son of God and the new kind of life that comes to those
who believe in him.

His dominant theme is that Jesus is the Son of God and knew
himself to be the Son of God from the very beginning. Jesus'
unique filial consciousness explains his power and his insight into
the will of God for men. We have already seen how the Synoptics
become more meaningful when the life and teaching of Jesus are
interpreted in the light of Jesus' filial consciousness. We found,
also, certain passages (cf. Matt. 11:27) that show how the Synoptic writers had this same insight into the inner consciousness of
Jesus. But that which is merely implicit throughout the Synoptics
becomes explicit in John, dominating his book from the first
chapter to the last.

In the majestic prologue (John 1:1-18), Jesus is presented as
the incarnate Word (Logos) of God. The "Logos" is a word

with a varied history and many different meanings. To Philo, the Alexandrine Jew, it meant the divine agent of creation; to Heraclitus it meant the divine reason; in Old Testament Judaism it stood for the creative revealing activity of God. The last mentioned is the central meaning for John. He expresses his faith in the revealing activity of God throughout all history and then states his Christian conviction that a historical person, Jesus Christ, is the incarnate expression of this divine revealing activity. The creative activity and thought of God, operative through all the ages, are now uniquely manifest in Jesus. Although the author does not specifically refer to this Logos principle after the prologue, his entire Gospel is an expansion of this theme.

The unique filial consciousness of Jesus, which the prologue explains in terms of the incarnate Word, is further developed throughout the Gospel in a series of well-known " I am " sayings that are not found in the Synoptics. In these passages the author attempts to state Jesus' own inner consciousness in a dramatic way. This is what Jesus knew himself to be in the depth of his own being. " I am the bread of life. . . . I am the light of the world. . . . I am the door of the sheep. . . . I am the good shepherd. . . . I am the true vine. . . . I am the resurrection and the life. . . . I am the way, and the truth, and the life." Since these are the things that Jesus essentially knew himself to be, the writer places the words on the lips of Jesus. The cumulative effect of these " I am " passages is particularly impressive when we read them all in the context of the author's attempt to plumb the depths of Jesus' own inner life.

This same inner filial consciousness is further expressed in Jesus' constant reference to himself as " the Son." In the Synoptic Gospels he called himself " the Son of man," using a Messianic title that he attempted to fill with new meaning. In John's Gospel he refers to himself as " the Son " in an obvious reference to the intimate love and dependent trust that he felt toward the Father. " The Son " is an expression of the deep consciousness of God that was the very secret of his being. It includes both the dependence and the intimacy that are part of a son's relationship to his father. Here again that which is lurking beneath the surface in the Synoptics is directly stated in John. In the former, Jesus knew himself to be the Son of God but chose a Messianic title. In John's Gospel everyone knows Jesus is the Messiah, but he primarily knows himself to be " the Son."

In other passages, Jesus says that he and the Father " are one," again emphasizing the sense of unity that he feels with the essential being of God. It should be noted, however, that Jesus is not referring to metaphysical unity between himself and God. This becomes clear when he prays that the disciples may have the same kind of unity that he has with the Father: " Holy Father, keep them in thy name which thou hast given me, that they may be one, even as we are one " (John 17:11). He is obviously referring, not to a metaphysical unity where the disciples lose their individuality, but to an intimate unity of sharing in understanding, purpose, and love. This is the kind of unity that Jesus felt between himself and God.

In these and other ways John develops his central theme. Because of his particular interest he has been called " the historian of the consciousness of Jesus." The other Gospels record the ministry and words of Jesus; John records his inner consciousness. This author is convinced that the life and teaching of Jesus are grounded in Jesus' own consciousness of Sonship with the Father. He places this conviction on the lips of Jesus because he is certain that this is a true reading of " the mind of Christ." This is partly what he meant when he said he wrote his Gospel in order that others might believe that " Jesus is the Christ, the Son of God."

C. ETERNAL LIFE

In the Gospel of John, eternal life is presented as the thing that the Son of God brings to men. In the Synoptics he proclaimed the good news of the reign of God, but in John the reign of God is defined as eternal life. Unfortunately, many persons think of eternal life primarily as a future life that begins after death. They describe it in terms of heaven and hell, heaven the reward for a good life here on earth, hell the punishment. In this scheme man's present life becomes a mere preparation for an eternal future life of joy or sorrow. Those who are wise will spend their time carefully preparing for the future.

Some time ago my wife and I met a man in the dining car of a speeding streamlined train. When we asked him about his work he replied that he was a salesman for a coffin manufacturer. He proceeded to describe his product in great detail, so enthusiastically we didn't have the heart to interrupt him. He concluded by saying that he was now selling coffins to people while they were still alive, moving the coffin into the attic or basement after the down payment had been made. It would be comforting, he insisted, to plan ahead in this way, to have the peace of mind that comes from knowing that our coffin has been purchased and is waiting for us. Then he began to laugh heartily, explaining that he wasn't really a coffin salesman at all but simply made up this story to help pass the time on his long trips, telling it to any gullible people who would listen! The joke was on us, but I thought afterward that the plan might really appeal to those people who spend so much time thinking and planning for eternal life as a future event that begins when the physical body dies.

We have emphasized this common view of eternal life in order to contrast it with the teaching of Jesus, who had something very different in mind. When he spoke of eternal life he was referring to a present quality of life rather than to a future event or place, to the reality of life as known here and now rather than to some speculative existence at an uncertain point in the future. "This is eternal life, that they know thee the only true God, and Jesus Christ whom thou hast sent." (John 17:3.) Eternal life is not a reward for virtue; it is the virtuous life itself. It is unconditional love of God, selfless obedience to him, fulfilling fellowship with him. When Jesus spoke of eternal life in terms of " knowing " God, he did not mean mere intellectual knowledge but that knowledge which is an act of the whole life, the whole personality. Eternal life, in short, is the appropriation of that quality of life which is inherent in God himself.

This means that eternal life is present and not future. It exists now, as Jesus implied by constantly referring to it in the present tense. It is a quality of life that becomes real to us now at this point of our temporal existence. At the same time it is a quality of life that is beyond time. Eternal life does not mean endless duration but existence in which we are lifted beyond or above the bounds of time.

Similarly, the judgment is not a future event in time, but a continuously present experience. " This is the judgment, that the light has come into the world, and men loved darkness rather than light, because their deeds were evil." (ch. 3:19.) " Now is the judgment of this world, now shall the ruler of this world be cast out." (ch. 12:31.) " Truly, I say to you, he who hears my word and believes him who sent me, has eternal life; he does not come into judgment, but has passed from death to life." (ch. 5:24.) In such statements Jesus is describing the judgment as a present spiritual experience in which we choose or reject eternal life. Judgment is that process of separating the good from the evil which is always in operation, intrinsic to life. Alienation from the quality of existence incarnate in Jesus is spiritual death; relatedness to that quality is eternal life. Thus a man's present attitude toward God and toward the Son is the decisive factor in the judgment.

This idea of judgment and eternal life as presented in the Fourth Gospel is foreign to the thought of many Christians, who think of themselves as " pilgrims passing through " this earthly life on the way to a heaven with streets of gold. But the author of this Gospel is convinced that eternal life as a present quality of existence is what Jesus was bringing to men when he proclaimed the good news of the reign of God. By thus adding eternal dimensions to man's present existence, Jesus made each present moment an event of momentous significance. The real meaning of heaven is caught up in this concept of an eternal life that is present now!

A great American preacher once said that every man needs two things — a home and a horizon. John's Gospel gives us both. Knowing Jesus as the Son of God, the author plumbs the depths of Jesus' inner consciousness in a search for man's true home in God. The meaning of life for Jesus and all men is in this kind of relatedness to the God who is incarnate in the Son. When a man discovers this true home, then he also inherits a horizon of " life " that reaches above time into eternity.

It is not difficult to see why the Fourth Gospel has been the most loved Gospel for countless Christians. By revealing the inner consciousness of Jesus, the author has made it possible for us to know the Son of God in the deep places of his own spirit. When John Knox was dying, he asked his wife to bring a Bible and read " the place where my soul first cast anchor." She knew exactly what he meant, and turning to the Gospel of John, she read the good news of a God who so loved the world that he gave his only Son in order that men might have eternal life. The Synoptics give us this Son as he was known to others. John gives us the Son as he was known to himself.

17

The Uniqueness of Jesus

In the summer of 1947, one of the most astounding discoveries of history was made in a cave near the Dead Sea. It all started the day a Bedouin shepherd boy threw a rock into a cave and ran away in fear when he heard the unexpected crash of breaking pottery. The next day he returned with a friend, and together they discovered the now famous Dead Sea scrolls. There were seven manuscripts in this first cave, one of them a copy of The Book of Isaiah one thousand years older than any other extant copy of that important Old Testament book! Since then other caves have yielded fragments of hundreds of other scrolls, all from a time that previously had been one of the most sparsely documented periods in man's history.

The narrative of the discovery, purchase, and translation of the scrolls reads like an exciting detective story. Those who first became aware of the value of the scrolls faced danger, intrigue, and almost insurmountable difficulties in trying to make them available for scholarly study. As the months passed, it became known that the scrolls were part of a library collected by a sect of Essenes who had a monastery in that area from 100 b.c. until the destruction of Jerusalem in a.d. 70. Since this period covers the life of Jesus and the birth of the early church, the discoveries are of inestimable value in the study of both Judaism and Christianity.

Public interest was first aroused when Edmund Wilson pub-

lished an article on the discovery in 1955, later expanding the
article into a book that instantly became a best seller. Countless
other articles and books appeared as excitement grew, stimulated
by many suggestions that this discovery would necessitate radical
changes in the basic faith of Christianity. Some persons were fear-
ful that the foundations of their faith would suddenly be shattered. Others were strangely eager to embarrass those whose faith
included beliefs and institutions different from their own.

The Essene writings featured a Teacher of Righteousness, a
leader of great strength and purity of life who felt that God had
called him to gather a group of Jerusalem priests and take them
into the desert. There he founded a closely knit community, in-
tending to remain until God established his Kingdom, when he
and his followers would become the nucleus of the New Israel.
In the first flurry of excitement after the discovery was announced, some journalists and scholars rushed into print with
the most startling conjectures. It was suggested that John the
Baptist was an Essene, that Jesus was an Essene, that Jesus derived his teaching from the Essenes, that the redemptive ministry
of Jesus was copied from the life of the Teacher of Righteousness.
The implication in every case was that Christ was not unique
after all, that his life and teaching could now be explained as a
product of social evolution.

Further study has established beyond doubt that the Dead Sea
scrolls in no way detract from the uniqueness of Jesus. On the
contrary, the contrast between Jesus and the Teacher of Righteousness becomes more obvious as scholarly study continues. It is
doubtful whether Jesus had direct contact of any kind with the
Essene group. They were ascetic, legalistic, ritualistic, and exclu-
sive. Jesus was exactly the opposite. Furthermore, there is no relationship between his teaching and theirs at any point. The
scrolls are extremely valuable in shedding new light on the period
of history in which Jesus lived, but they have enhanced rather
than destroyed the uniqueness of Jesus.

Still, the problem of his uniqueness remains for those who know him. The early Christians were convinced that he was far more than a great prophet returned. He was the Son of God. Christians in every age have shared this conviction, but they have often been unable to explain it. The embarrassment and anxiety of many church members during the earliest discussions of the Dead Sea scrolls pointed up a serious weakness. Unable to explain their conviction about the uniqueness of Jesus, many persons retreated in fear and " blind faith."

This question arises in every generation and it must be honestly faced. Adherents of other religions want to know. Nonbelievers want to know. Honest and curious young people want to know. Troubled church members want to know. What is meant by saying that Jesus was the Son of God and therefore utterly unique?

A. LIFE AND TEACHING

The total impression left by the life of Jesus is that of its unique value in revealing the nature of God. This is not to say that he has not been revealed through the lives of others, through a Paul, an Augustine, a Francis of Assisi. But no other life even approaches the wholeness, vividness, and influence of the divine revelation that occurred through the life of Jesus. Men in every generation have been convinced that in this life and through this life they see God as they are able to see him in no other way.

This is partly because the life of Jesus was a perfect embodiment of his own teaching about the nature of God and his reign. Jesus emphasized the will of God in his teaching, at the same time fully and joyfully accepting it for his own life. From beginning to end, through temptation, suffering, and the agony of Gethsemane, this was his dominant desire: " Nevertheless, not my will, but thine, be done." He demonstrated, further, how obedience to the will of God often spells itself out in terms of creative, redemptive, unselfish love for others. This was his teaching and this was his life. Love for sinners, for the lonely, for the lost, for the sick, for the sorrowing, for the hungry of body, and for the hungryhearted!

In everyone else there is a wide gulf between the ideal and the actual. Not so with Jesus. His whole life was of one piece, utterly obedient to the will of God. In this sense his life was a unique revelation of God's will for men.

Likewise, the teaching that grew out of the life and that was embodied in the life is a unique revelation of God. It is true that most of his ideas and sayings can be paralleled by those of the scribes and teachers of Judaism, as great Jewish scholars such as Rabbi Klausner have made quite clear. But those who reject the teaching of Jesus because his sayings were not original miss the main point. Jesus took ideas that had been glimpsed by those who preceded him and wove them into a unity or whole that is unique in the history of human thought. The Lord's Prayer is an example. Each separate part has a parallel in Judaism, but there is no parallel for the tremendous effect of the prayer as a whole. The same may be said for all his teaching. He knew what to leave out and what to include in weaving a unique coherent portrait of the Kingdom of God.

His teaching is also unmatched in its intensity and authority. Its power in this respect grew out of his own sense of filial consciousness to God. He spoke as no other man has spoken because he spoke out of an unparalleled sense of oneness with God. The influence of his teaching is also unmatched in history. No other teacher has been so effective in changing the lives of men and the course of human destiny. The total impression left by his teaching is therefore the same as that left by his life. Here is a unique revelation of God, unique in its completeness, its vividness, its authority, its influence.

Those who wish to explain the uniqueness of Jesus may start with his life and teaching. Either alone is an intensely vivid revelation of the nature of God and his reign. Taken together, they reveal the truth about God so completely that his followers speak with burning joy and contagious enthusiasm of the fullness of God shining in the face of Jesus.

B. DEATH AND RESURRECTION

Two events in the life of Jesus further contribute to his uniqueness. The first of these is his redemptive death. We have already emphasized his originality in applying the concept of the Suffering Servant to his own Messianic ministry. This was utterly new in the thought of Judaism, where both the idea of the Messiah and that of the Suffering Servant had a significant history. No one had thought to combine them until Jesus said that God's anointed one would come as one who served and suffered. The idea that suffering could be redemptive and the idea that the Messiah's ministry would be fulfilled through suffering was so unique that the contemporaries of Jesus nailed him on a cross for suggesting it!

Here on the cross the redemptive suffering of the Messiah reached a unique climax. Other men have died as martyrs; other men have died for their friends. No other death has had the influence on history that the death of Jesus had. His teaching and his life reached a climax at the moment of his death.

Christians have tried to describe the meaning of his death in the doctrine of the atonement. As we have already seen, many men were certain they had become reconciled (at one) with God because of Christ's death. Those who have experienced this reconciliation cannot agree in describing or explaining it, but they all agree on what it has meant for their lives. Formerly estranged from God and utterly unable to break down the wall of separation that left them in a state of despair, they discovered that the wall had already been broken down through the redemptive death of Jesus. This was the holy surprise made possible by the grace of God. The fact that Jesus died is not unique, but the circumstances and results of his death are utterly unique.

Similarly unique, and even more incredible, is the fact that the agonizing death on the cross did not end Jesus' life. From the moment the unbelievable report of his resurrection first spread, the life of Jesus has been distinguished by this unparalleled event. Plunged into the lowest depths of despair by his death, the disciples suddenly " knew " that he was alive. This was not something they began to believe about him, but something they experienced as individuals and in groups. There is overwhelming evidence to support our own certainty that Jesus was known by his friends after his death and that he is known still in the community of faith.

Unfortunately, many persons become entangled in the thorny unresolved questions surrounding the resurrection event. What was the nature of the resurrection body? What happened to the physical body? It must be emphasized again that there can be lack of agreement on these questions even while still affirming the important fact! The living Lord was known by the early disciples and he is known still.

In the resurrection, God broke into history to reverse the decision of the cross. He authenticated through this event the life, teaching, and redemptive death of his own Son. This is God's way of validating the ministry of Jesus and his message of good news. No other figure in history has had his work authenticated in this way. No other human person has overcome death in this way. No other teacher lives on in quite the way Jesus lives on. This event is utterly unique because God has chosen this way of saying to men, " This is my beloved Son; listen to him."

Every time a Christian attends worship on Sunday, or reads the New Testament, or joins in the celebration of the Eucharist, or seeks the meaning of the church's life, he runs into the resurrection as an event that strengthens his conviction that Jesus Christ is Lord alone. Many great figures of past history are remembered with reverence and esteem. No other figure of history is known still as a living Lord.

C. The Christ Event

It is possible to summarize this whole matter in one sentence: Jesus Christ is unique because he is God's unique act in history. When we speak of him as God's act we mean the entire Christ event, including the person (his life, teaching, death, and resurrection) and the community of faith that grew out of man's experience of the person. In this event the supreme revealing act of God takes place as God makes himself known to men. This is not something man has done but something God has done. God himself has chosen to act in this way.

This revealing act of God, which we call the Christ event, is God's unique act in history. He has revealed himself in an infinite number of other ways. He has revealed himself through other persons in other religions. But the Christian is convinced that these are all partial and imperfect compared with the Christ event. Only here is he known as the " God and Father of our Lord Jesus Christ." This is to know him in a unique way.

This is to know him also in the way the first disciples knew him. It is possible to spend so much time debating about the fine points of Christology that we forget the impression that Christ first made. He was something that happened to the disciples, a historical event that they experienced. In this event they were certain that God had acted, taking the initiative in revealing himself. Later they described this experience in the doctrine of the incarnation, trying to say that in Jesus the divine creative activity had taken on flesh to dwell among them. God took on flesh in a particular person who became the center of a particular event that is his supreme revealing act in man's life. This revealing act is the center of history because it gives meaning to all of history and reveals God's purpose for history.

There is a famous old story about a sculptor who called in a group of children to view a partially finished statue. " Oh," they exclaimed, " it is a great man." The sculptor sent them away and continued his work. When he called them again they said, " It is a good man." The sculptor worked longer and called them a third time. This time they said, " It is Jesus," and he was satisfied. Christians are certain that Jesus is not just a great man or a good man. He is Jesus the Christ, God's unique act in history.

Unfortunately, this Christian conviction has led to tragic misunderstanding between Christians and members of other religions. Some church members, consciously and subconsciously, have given non-Christians the impression that Christ is God's *only* revealing act in history and that those who have not known God through Christ have not known him at all. Paul knew better, pointing out that God has not left himself without witness among any people. It would be far better to rejoice with others in the revelation of God that has come to them, and then go on to share with them the unspeakable joy of knowing God through Christ. How many persons have rejected the unsearchable riches of Christ because of the arrogant dogmatic attitude of certain of his followers who have not learned to love!

Even more tragic is the dissension among Christians themselves. From the beginning, those who have been privileged to participate in God's unique revealing act in Christ have attacked one another mercilessly because of differences in doctrine, ritual, and church government. We have burned fellow Christians at the stake, literally and figuratively, because we could not force them into the particular doctrinal mold that suited us.

This dissension would be tragic in any age. In the twentieth century it has become fatal. For the first time in history man has the power to destroy himself. The only power strong enough to prevent him from doing this is the power of God revealed in the unique Christ event. But God's power in Christ goes without witness because Christians are too busy fighting among themselves! In Boston several years ago I witnessed a strange scene when a small building housing a chemical firm caught fire. Fed by the chemicals, the flames shot upward in a spectacular display of dancing colors. Several fire companies had drawn their equipment up around the building and were shooting streams of water toward the center of the fire. The strange thing was that they were fooled by the height of the flames and were aiming too high. Most of them were directing their hoses over the top of the building, drenching the firemen on the other side! It took them several minutes to correct the difficulty and unite their efforts in fighting the fire. God's unique act in Christ is the only power strong enough to fight the flames of destruction threatening civilization. Tragically, however, Christians have been spending their time drenching one another rather than uniting to fight the fire. The least we could do, in view of man's tragic dilemma, is to learn to disagree in love!

The unsearchable riches of Christ are now man's only hope for himself and for his civilization. This is because the Christ event is not a human answer to the predicament of individuals and society. We have tried all the human answers and they have failed. The Christ event is God's answer, his own unique revealing act in history. Christ is the way to God, the truth about God, the life of God among men. Man can never save himself. He can only be saved from himself through the reconciling Christ event in which God reveals himself to his own children as a loving Father who rejoices when they turn and come home to him.

APPENDIX

For Further Study

THE APPENDIX to John's Gospel ends with the following statement: "There are also many other things which Jesus did; were every one of them to be written, I suppose that the world itself could not contain the books that would be written." One wonders what this author might say if he were alive today to witness the ever-increasing numbers of books on Jesus that continue to appear. The amazing thing is that nearly every one sheds some new light on the old story.

This book is intended as an introduction to the life and teaching of Jesus for the student and general reader. We have attempted to present the material in a direct and orderly manner so that it stands as a complete story in itself but also points the way to further study. The following methods of procedure are suggested for those who wish to use this book as a guide for advanced study.

A. THE GOSPELS

Most persons will find a systematic examination of the Gospel texts the best method of gaining further knowledge in this field. Highly recommended as a basic tool is a copy of the *Gospel Parallels* in the Revised Standard Version (Thomas Nelson & Sons, 1949). This provides the student with the complete text of the Synoptic Gospels in parallel columns, thus making it unnecessary to leaf back and forth while examining any given incident or teaching. Invaluable also in Gospel study is *The Interpreter's Bible,* Vols. 7 to 8 (Abingdon Press, 1951). This work provides introductory articles and detailed commentary, prepared by outstanding scholars, on every passage in the Gospels. Similarly helpful is *The Mission and Message of Jesus,* by Major, Manson, and Wright (E. P. Dutton & Co., Inc., 1938). Also highly recommended are *The Westminster Historical Atlas to the Bible,* by Wright and Filson (The Westminister Press, rev. ed., 1956), and *Harper's Bible Dictionary* (Harper & Brothers, 1952).

Biblical references have been made throughout this book. Those wishing to develop a program of further study may therefore use all of the above reference tools in a careful examination of the Gospels. This method of procedure is especially fruitful since the Gospels are the primary sources on which every study of the life and teaching of Jesus is ultimately based.

B. Interpretations of the Gospels

Outstanding interpretations of the Gospels have been prepared by scholars of many persuasions. Students seeking further information may secure one or more of these books and make use of the suggestions for additional reading that have been made below for each chapter of this book.

Dwight Beck, *Through the Gospels to Jesus* (Harper & Brothers, 1954), discusses the texts of the Gospels with much helpful historical detail. Maurice Goguel, *The Life of Jesus* (The Macmillan Company, 1933), is a carefully balanced and appreciative biography, perhaps the best scholarly life of Jesus to date. Edgar Goodspeed, *A Life of Jesus* (Harper & Brothers, 1950), is a popular and readable study, the fruit of a lifetime of sound scholarship. Charles Guignebert, *Jesus* (University Books, Inc., 1956), critically sifts the traditions about Jesus to the bare historical bones. A. M. Hunter, *The Work and Words of Jesus* (The Westminster Press, 1950), is extremely helpful in interpreting the mission of Jesus. Howard C. Kee and Franklin W. Young, *Understanding the New Testament* (Prentice-Hall, Inc., 1957), place Jesus and the Gospels in the perspective of the whole New Testament. Charles M. Laymon, *The Life and Teachings of Jesus* (Abingdon Press, 1955), is a helpful systematic approach to the Gospel material. Vincent Taylor, *The Life and Ministry of Jesus* (Abingdon Press, 1955), includes many of the finest fruits of modern New Testament interpretation.

C. OTHER HELPFUL BOOKS

Branscomb, Harvie, *The Teachings of Jesus*. Abingdon Press, 1931. A careful analysis of the major teachings of Jesus.

Cadoux, Cecil J., *The Historic Mission of Jesus*. Harper & Brothers, 1943. Scholarly examination of the problem of eschatology.

Deane, Anthony C., *The World Christ Knew*. Michigan State College, 1953. Re-placing Jesus in his own time.

Eiselen, F. C., ed., *The Abingdon Bible Commentary*. Abingdon Press, 1929. One of the best and most widely used one-volume commentaries.

Fosdick, Harry E., *The Man from Nazareth*. Harper & Brothers, 1949. Jesus as his contemporaries saw him. An unusual approach.

Johnson, Sherman E., *Jesus in His Homeland*. Charles Scribner's Sons, 1957. Re-placing Jesus in his own environment.

Kepler, Thomas S., ed., *Contemporary Thinking About Jesus*. Abingdon Press, 1944. Well-chosen passages from some fifty modern scholars, making an anthology on several phases of the life and teaching of Jesus.

Klausner, Joseph, *Jesus of Nazareth*, tr. by Herbert Danby. The Macmillan Company, 1925. Jesus as seen by a Jewish rabbi. The most valuable portrait of Jesus the Jew by a Jew.

Knox, John, *Jesus, Lord and Christ*. Harper & Brothers, 1958. An excellent study of Christology.

Laymon, Charles M., *The Life and Teachings of Jesus*. Abingdon Press, 1955. A brief introduction to the problems in this field.

Lebreton, Jules, *The Life and Teaching of Jesus Christ Our Lord*, tr. by Francis Day. Bruce Publishing Company, 1935. A readable Roman Catholic view by a Jesuit scholar of distinction.

Olmstead, Albert T., *Jesus in the Light of History*. Charles Scribner's Sons, 1942. A noted scholar writes with assurance about chronology and other details of the life of Jesus.

Rollins, W. E. and M. B., *Jesus and His Ministry*. The Seabury Press, Inc., 1954. A balanced popular study.

Schweitzer, Albert, *The Mystery of the Kingdom of God*, tr. by Walter Lowrie. The Macmillan Company, 1950. This famous author's eschatological interpretation of Jesus.

Simkhovitch, Vladimir G., *Toward the Understanding of Jesus*. The Macmillan Company, 1947. A famous little essay placing

Jesus amid the revolutionary tensions of his time.

Stewart, James S., *The Life and Teaching of Jesus Christ*. Abingdon Press, 1950. A popular presentation including helpful questions for study and discussion.

Tilden, Elwyn E., *Toward Understanding Jesus*. Prentice-Hall, Inc., 1956. A helpful introduction to the problems that must be faced in any study of Jesus.

Wilder, Amos N., *Eschatology and Ethics in the Teaching of Jesus*. Harper & Brothers, 1950. A very helpful discussion of the important problem suggested in the title.

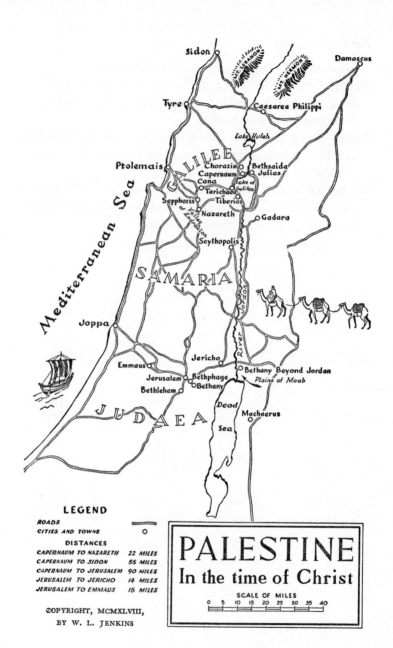

LEGEND

ROADS ——————

CITIES AND TOWNS   ○

DISTANCES

CAPERNAUM TO NAZARETH   22 MILES
CAPERNAUM TO SIDON   55 MILES
CAPERNAUM TO JERUSALEM   90 MILES
JERUSALEM TO JERICHO   14 MILES
JERUSALEM TO EMMAUS   15 MILES

PALESTINE
In the time of Christ

SCALE OF MILES

0 5 10 15 20 25 30 35 40

Index

Q document, 37–38, 197

Reconciliation, 105, 107, 170–179
Reign of God. *See* Kingdom of God
Religion of the Jews, 26–28
Repentance, 175–176
Resurrection of Jesus. *See* Jesus Christ
Resuscitation, 71–72
Roman Empire, 21, 23–24

Sabbath, 79, 114
Sacrifice, 27
Sadducees, 28, 91
Salvation. *See* Reconciliation
Samaritans, 19, 84
Sanhedrin, 101, 108
Satan, 81
Schweitzer, Albert, 48, 162, 194
Scribes, 78, 92, 128
Sermon on the Mount, 40, 191–193
Service, 188–189
Seven Last Words, 104–105
Shekinah, 82
Shema, 135
Sin, 172–173
Sincerity, 188
Socrates, 126
Solomon, 25, 137
Son of God, 52–54, 199–204, 211–213, 217–225
Son of man, 198

Sources
  pagan, 32–33
  Jewish, 33
  Christian, 33, 34
Streeter, B. H., 36–37
Substitutionary atonement, 105–106
Suetonius, 33
Suffering Servant, 73, 103, 155–156, 198–199, 221
Sunday, 114
Synagogues, 27
Synoptic Gospels, 35, 208
Synoptic problem, 36–39

Tacitus, 32
Talmud, 33
Temple, 27, 88–90
Temptations of Jesus. *See* Jesus Christ
Thomas, 74, 110, 113
Thomas, Gospel of, 33
Tillich, Paul, 107
Torah. *See* Law
Transfiguration, 81–83
Trial of Jesus. *See* Jesus Christ

Via Dolorosa, 103
Virgin birth, 46, 51–54

Youth of Jesus. *See* Jesus Christ

Zacchaeus, 85
Zealots, 23, 29, 151–152
Zechariah, 88